DESCENT INTO LOVE

DESCENT INTO
LOVE

HOW RECOVERY CAFÉ
CAME TO BE

K. KILLIAN NOE

All of the proceeds from the sale of this book
support Recovery Café in its mission to welcome
women and men who have suffered homelessness,
addiction and other mental health challenges into a
community where they come to know they are loved
and that they have gifts to share.

inward outward
Washington, DC

*All of the proceeds from the sale of this book go to
support Recovery Café.*

Edited by Kim I. Montroll
Cover and book design by J. Martin Saunders

Cover photography by Peter Yates

Permission for previously published material has been
requested.

First edition

inward/outward
The Church of the Saviour
1640 Columbia Road, NW
Washington, DC 20009

inwardoutwardeditor@gmail.com
www.inwardoutward.org

ISBN: 978-0-692-52220-2

There is no way to mention by name all the Recovery Café Members, staff, board, volunteers, donors, members of New Creation Community and others who have participated in the life of Recovery Café community since its inception. Each of you has given the immeasurable gift of yourself and none of us will ever be the same. Our gratitude for you is too deep for words. All Recovery Café Members' names have been changed to honor anonymity.

Until one is committed, there is hesitancy, the chance to draw back, always ineffectiveness, concerning all acts of initiative [and creation]. There is one elementary truth in ignorance of which kills countless ideas and splendid plans: that the moment one definitely commits oneself, then Providence moves too. All sorts of things occur to help one that would never otherwise have occurred. A whole stream of events issues from the decision, raising in one's favor all manner of unforeseen incidents and meetings and material assistance which no man could have dreamed would have come his way. Whatever you can do or dream you can, begin it. Boldness has genius, power and magic in it. Begin it now.

Johann Wolfgang von Goethe

CONTENTS

INTRODUCTION

The following stories about the founding of Recovery Café are told from the perspective of the author. Without her vision of a healing community where people from radically different life experiences gather and discover that they "belong to each other," Recovery Café would not exist.

Killian has the gift of drawing people into a vision, all kinds of people. As her long-time friend in Washington, DC, Mike Little, says: "Be careful if you are sitting next to Killian because she will draw you into something."

In Killian's deepest core is a desire to connect with the place of Divine Love in herself and in every person she meets; a desire to live with a conscious awareness of oneness with God and with the entire human family.

What flows from that desire for unitive consciousness is a desire to close the gap between those who have what they need to fulfill their potential and those who do not, and her belief that small, authentic communities that cross racial, socio-economic, religious and other barriers can be transformative for all involved. For over thirty years she has been relentless in her commitment to nurturing such communities, including Samaritan Inns in DC, for women and men recovering from homelessness and addiction.

She has been inspired by communities she has visited or spent time with all over the world such as: Missionaries of Charity in Calcutta, Trappists on Lantau Island in Hong Kong Harbor, Maryknolls in Nicaragua, Taizé in France, the Johweto community, committed to racial reconciliation in South Africa, and eighteen years at the ecumenical Church of the Saviour in

Washington, DC. Much of what she has learned from these communities and from the communities in which she has grounded herself is reflected in the following pages.

"Killian identifies so strongly with the suffering," says Recovery Café co-founder Mary Crow, "and believed that if we did the footwork then God would move with us and Recovery Café would come to be. Her deep faith that everything we needed to fulfill the vision would be given, her love for people from all walks of life, her capacity to see and call forth the gifts of others, her irreverent sense of humor and her infectious joy, encouraged us and taught us that the impossible is possible."

Board member Dr. Vicki Allen, a primary care physician in downtown Seattle, shares, "Recovery Café heals what ails so many in our society—loneliness, mental illness, addiction, trauma—offering unconditional love. For many, this may be the first time they experience community and acceptance. It does not matter who you are, what you have done, what has happened to you, whether you are off the streets or here to donate, you are treated with the same love and respect. It is such a feeling of acceptance and love, it is transformative, it is curative. The Café heals wounds like no other program."

Grounded in authentic local community, Killian has a deep desire for her life and the Recovery Café model to be part of eradicating the stigma associated with addiction and other mental health challenges, and reforming the criminal justice system that imprisons women and men suffering from addiction and other mental health challenges. She envisions, instead, healing communities, like Recovery Café, in every town and city across the U.S. where the addicted and mentally anguished can reclaim their lives.

"Killian locates herself and finds her deepest joy with those who have been most excluded and cast-out in our society, and draws others in," said long-time friend Kim Montroll. "In her life and in this book, she calls all of us to stand in the gap, the place of greatest pain, hope and healing."

As we read, **Descent into Love** draws us into the journeys of remarkable people, from many streams of life, flowing into one stream of love—the essence of Recovery Café.

Ruby Takushi, Ph.D.
Co-Founder and Director of Programs, *Recovery Café*

David Coffey
Executive Director, *Recovery Café*

1

STORY BEFORE
THE STORY

The one journey that ultimately matters is the journey into the place of stillness deep within one's self. To reach that place is to be at home; to fail to reach it is to be forever restless. In contemplation we catch a vision of not only what is, but what can be. Contrary to what we have thought, contemplatives are the great doers.

N. Gordon Cosby

We try so hard to hang on to the teachings and "get it," but actually the truth sinks in like rain into very hard earth. The rain is very gentle, and we soften up slowly at our own speed. But when that happens, something has fundamentally changed in us. That hard earth has softened. It doesn't seem to happen by trying to get it or capture it. It happens by letting go; it happens by relaxing your mind, and it happens by the aspiration and the longing to want to communicate with yourself and others. Each of us finds our own way... Let everything stop your mind and let everything open your heart.

Pema Chodron

SURROUNDED by towering evergreens in Canada's Bay of Fundy National Park, I found the silence was deafening. I had left our campsite for a solitary run to escape the tension between Bernie and me over whether or not he would accept the job he wanted in Seattle.

As I ran I tried to visualize leaving the people I loved in Washington, DC and began to cry so hard I couldn't breathe. I am not talking about the kind of tears that gently streak your cheeks until they glisten. I'm talking about the kind of crying that makes your eyes puffy, your nose runny and your breath desperate.

Since I could not manage to take in enough oxygen to run and cry at the same time, I found a boulder and sat down. That's when I heard the voice. It wasn't an audible voice but it was strong and clear and seemed to be coming from some place deep inside of me. It said, "Let go and trust."

I spoke out loud to the forest, as if God was hiding behind one of the evergreens, "God, if that's you, why don't you tell Bernie 'to let go and trust?'"

But there was only silence.

"God, please don't tell me you are the sexist that religious people for centuries have made you out to be. Please don't tell me I have to leave the work and people I love just because my husband wants to move."

I thought of the old saying, "God made us in his own image and we keep trying to return the favor." We project onto God our limitations, our narrow-mindedness, our biases, our anger, our violence. The God we create in our own image is small and petty and, not surprisingly, thinks like we think.

Aware of the noisy, theological rant going on in my head, I tried to return to the silence.

Soon I realized I had stopped crying and could continue my run. When I got back to the campsite I told Bernie in a flat voice, "I'll move to Seattle." Later I explained that I had agreed to move, not because I believed my husband's call automatically trumped my call. I had agreed to move because, as best as I could discern, I had been given guidance to that effect.

Everyone tells her story from her own perspective, which is inevitably a partial view of the whole. This is my partial view.

For eighteen years prior to that particular guidance, I had been deeply rooted in the ecumenical Church of the Saviour in Washington, DC, a community lived out in distinct cell communities. Gordon Cosby, the founder and pastor, died in 2013 at age ninety-five. He was a spiritual father, mentor and friend to me for over thirty years.

At the Church of the Saviour I learned about contemplation and action, the inward and outward journey. I learned that by rigorously pursuing the inward journey—a deepening connection with our truest self, with God and with others in authentic community—we discover our outward journey, where our gifts connect with some need or suffering in the world. Gordon emphasized that "unless one's outward call flows from the depths of one's inner being, it will have limited power to heal and transform."

The notion that our "doing" must flow from the depths of our "being" and that we must stay grounded in those depths—even as we move into the suffering of the world—was not a new understanding. A similar challenge was given to Arjuna in the Bhagavad Gita, written sometime between the fifth century BCE and the first century CE. Arjuna is standing on the battlefield, reflecting on the carnage and anguish all around him when he is instructed, "Plunge into the heat of the battle, but keep your heart at the lotus feet of the Lord."

At the Church of the Saviour, I experienced authentic community as the place where we are both known and loved; as the place we practice forgiving ourselves and others; as the place we are held to spiritual practices that keep our hearts open to transforming love.

It was in the soil of the Church of the Saviour community that David Erickson and I both heard and responded to a call to create healing communities in DC, named Samaritan Inns, where homeless, addicted and mentally anguished women and men who had fallen through the cracks of our society could reclaim and rebuild their lives.

It was in that same soil that we came to understand that if we are loving our "neighbors" deeply enough, we will be drawn into helping dismantle systems that oppress and exclude those we've come to love.

In 1993, Samaritan Inns purchased another old, run-down apartment building to be transformed into our second drug and alcohol-free housing community. We had obtained the appropriate construction permits and construction was well underway when city officials stormed onto our property and shut down construction.

We soon discovered that we had not violated any city codes; rather the neighbors had put so much pressure on the city to keep the women and men we served out of their neighborhood that the city officials had caved under the pressure.

To make a long, four-year story short, Samaritan Inns ended up suing the District of Columbia for violation of the fair housing laws of the Civil Rights Act. The case ended up in federal court in a thirteen-day trial. At the end of the trial, the Honorable Richard Urbina ruled that the District of Columbia had, in fact, acted in gross violation of the fair housing laws by knowingly discriminating against the women and men Samaritan Inns served. We resumed construction and opened a beautiful forty-five-unit apartment building.

Here's the irony. Because our residents are rigorously committed to their recovery, our building is the only apartment building in the neighborhood in which there are absolutely no drugs being used or sold. This precedent-setting case has been used by non-profits all over the country to fight discrimination against various groups being denied housing.

It's important to note that we did not just wake up one morning and decide we wanted to spend the next four years embroiled in legal battles. Our willingness to enter this fight grew out of long-standing, authentic relationships with the women and men who were being denied housing. In other words, our call to fight *for* those being excluded grew out of our call to be in relationship **with** those being excluded.

Our pro bono attorney, John Risher—without whom we would not have won this battle—was one of the most celebrated trial lawyers in one of the most prestigious law firms in Washington, DC. What we did not know during this four-year battle is that our case would be one of the last cases Mr. Risher would ever argue. He died unexpectedly, not too long after the ruling on our case. At his funeral his grieving widow shared, "I want you to know, fighting for justice on behalf of the women and men Samaritan Inns serves was the most meaningful and joyful work of my husband's thirty-six-year career."

• • •

Finding a spiritual home as an adult had not been easy for me. I had grown up in North and South Carolina, the daughter of a kind, Southern Baptist minister and a feisty, good-hearted mother. I struggled to hold together clear answers with paradox and mystery. Only our hearts can hold mystery and paradox and I was more and more drawn to live from my heart.

When I left home for Wake Forest University, I left behind the church of my childhood and attended an African-American church with Odessa, the maid who cleaned my college dorm. The sermons that drew heavily on the themes of exile and "speaking truth to power" awakened a sense of urgency in me. Even though I was as white as the Easter lilies on the church altar, I identified with the feeling of being an outsider. I attribute that alienation in part to existential despair common for that age and in part to an innate awareness of my belonging to those who were marginalized in the dominant culture in which I was raised.

That sense of being different and not fitting in continued to deepen in me throughout college. When I graduated I headed to the Middle East to serve with the Journeymen, a two-year volunteer service commitment like Jesuit Volunteer Corps and the Peace Corps.

My volunteer assignment was outside Tel Aviv, but I often visited the Fitzgeralds, who ran a hospital for Palestinian refugees in the Gaza Strip. I loved to help out around the hospital and once was even allowed to stand beside Dr. Fitzgerald as he removed a Palestinian boy's appendix. Often Dr. Fitzgerald was called upon to remove deeply embedded pieces of shrapnel and bullets from Palestinians who had grown up, as had generations before them, in the nearby refugee camp.

One Saturday, I left the hospital compound to pick up

a falafel in pita from the stand across the street. As I turned away from the falafel stand a grenade thrown at an Israeli military vehicle exploded, killing two Palestinians. One man's body flew by me, propelled by the explosion. His head splattered like a watermelon dropped on hot pavement. Everything seemed to be in slow motion as I made my way back to the hospital compound, which was soon overrun by Israeli soldiers. They believed the person who threw the bomb at their military vehicle was hiding in the hospital compound.

Still operating in slow motion, I crawled into a large garbage container, watched and waited as members of the Israeli Defense Force methodically kicked in every hospital room door, in search of the one who threw the grenade.

My journal entry that night, February 7, 1981, expressed a new realization for me: "If the Israelis and Palestinians—who have pain and fear, hopes and dreams, just like me—can hate each other so intensely that they literally blow each other to pieces, I, too, must be capable of that kind of hatred. If I am capable of such profound hatred, am I not also capable of more profound love than I have ever experienced?"

I discovered I needed a larger framework for my spiritual life and that I longed for a deeper experience with reconciling, unconditional love, a love more profound than religious and cultural divides and warring nations.

Contemplative Thomas Merton writes: "All through the *Verba Seniorum (Stories of the Desert Fathers and Mothers)* we find a repeated insistence on the primacy of love over everything else in the spiritual life: over knowledge, gnosis, asceticism, contemplation, solitude, prayer. Love, in fact, *is* the spiritual life, and without it all the other exercises of the spirit, however lofty, are emptied of content and become mere illusions. The more lofty they are, the more dangerous the illusion."

Theologian Karen Armstrong says it this way, "The religious traditions were in unanimous agreement. The one and only test of a valid religious idea, doctrinal statement, spiritual experience, or devotional practice was that it must lead directly to practical compassion. If your understanding of the divine made you kinder, more empathetic, and impelled you to express this sympathy in concrete acts of loving-kindness, this was good theology. But if your notion of God made you unkind, belligerent, cruel or self-righteous, or if it led you to kill in God's name, it was bad theology. Compassion was the litmus test."

We all have within us the capacity for great evil and great love. We all reflect shadow and light. And we all, either consciously or unconsciously, project onto others some of our shadow and some of our light.

The spiritual journey requires a deepening awareness of our own shadow and light. It requires a rigorous commitment to "catching ourselves in the act" of automatic, programmed responses. It requires choosing instead to respond from the place of light in us and to call forth that light in every life we touch. It requires a descent into our deepest, truest self, into the wellspring of Divine Love in us. That descent involves a thousand deaths to the ego, a constant pattern of letting go and surrendering at deeper and deeper levels. The descent often involves suffering which we do not choose–it chooses us–and some consistent practice of returning to our center, like contemplative prayer and meditation.

> *I must never lose sight of those other deaths which precede the final, physical death, the deaths over which we have some freedom; the death of self-will, self-indulgence, self-deception, all those self-devices which, instead of making us more fully alive, make us less. The times I have been most fully me are when I have been wholly involved in someone or something else; when I am listening, rather than talking; cooking a special, festive dinner, struggling with a fugue at the piano; putting a baby to bed; writing. A long-dead philosopher said that if we practice dying enough during our lives we will hardly notice the moment of transition when the actual time comes.*
> —Madeleine L'Engle

The spiritual descent into Divine Love–the recovery journey–may be prompted by suffering, spiritual practices/intentions and love, but we cannot steer or control our descent. Our intentions are like gates we desire to pass through. Once we've passed through, however, we look back and see that there were no gates. This descent, or free fall, may follow a course similar to the stages below, but it is not a linear journey. We cycle through the various stages over and over again. Perhaps each time something in us is transformed. We inevitably transmit to others both what gets transformed and what does not get transformed, which gives urgency and importance to this inner work. I've tried to describe these stages even though they are literally too deep for words. My description is based in part on my own experience and the experience of countless others—both members of Recovery Café and those from radically different realities—who have shared their "descent" with me.

Stages of Spiritual Descent into Love

Stage 1:   Our identity is based largely on external

realities like what we do or don't do, what we own or don't own, what we like or dislike, how we look or don't look, how we think others perceive us and how we perceive ourselves in ways that are good or bad.

Stage 2: There is beginning recognition of an inner hunger and a recognition that seeking to fill that inner hunger with more and more external things, activities or distractions simply doesn't work.

Stage 3: There is beginning capacity to observe our own behaviors. Those behaviors confront some of our ideas about ourselves, both good and bad. Although our identity is still rooted in our surface self or "false self," a shift begins to take place.

Stage 4: We begin to "look under the hood" of our ego structure, observe behavior patterns and even connect those patterns to earlier periods of our lives. We begin to get in touch with underlying emotions and energies such as rage, fear, self-loathing, shame and habitual blame.

Stage 5:   We experience grief, remorse and a sense of our profound inadequacy. We are aware that nothing we do can set us free from the attachment to our ego, or false self, and the behaviors that emerge from that construct. Some mystics have referred to this stage as the "Dark Night of the Soul."

Stage 6:   There is an awareness of a need for constant surrender or "letting go" of the need for control, need for approval, need to numb or dissociate from pain, need to make ourselves secure.

Stage 7:   There is an experience of diminished longing that is a stark contrast to the conscious and unconscious longing that has been present our entire lives. There is a peace that the material world cannot give and cannot take away. There is an experience of oneness, of not being separate from God or from any other member of the human family. While most earlier longing has diminished, one longing has intensified, to experience and manifest Love.

•   •   •

On our first Saturday after moving to Seattle I met Randall Mullins for coffee. Randall was a United Church of Christ pastor who had long dreamed of starting a church in Seattle in the tradition of the Church of the Saviour in DC. His brother-in-law, who served on the search committee that offered Bernie the job as Head of Lakeside School, had connected us.

Even though I had agreed to move to Seattle, I was still raw from having been uprooted from my faith community and from my community at Samaritan Inns. For fifteen years at Samaritan Inns, I had the privilege of accompanying hundreds of "outsiders" as they reclaimed their lives, became part of community, regained health, got married, raised children and contributed to the larger DC community. I could have taken a vow of stability, like some monks do, and spent the rest of my life with these communities of authentic, beautiful, broken, grateful and often hilarious people—what Henri Nouwen calls "wounded healers."

Certain that Randall could not possibly have envisioned a community like the precious community I had just left, I asked him, "Randall, how about writing down nine or ten spiritual practices members would gather around if you and I were to start a new faith community?"

While Randall was writing, I decided I would do the same, even though I seriously doubted we would find ourselves in the same hemisphere. After some twenty minutes of scribbling, we traded our answer sheets and began reading what the other had written. When we had both finished we looked at each other with astonishment. We had written exactly the same nine commitments we felt were essential in the faith community we longed for and needed. The order was not exactly the same, but that had not been part of the assignment.

What we both understood is that we wanted to create a "go" community rather than a "come" community. Some churches spend much of their energy and resources on getting people to "come" to their church. Getting people to come is important because you can't have community without people, but getting people to come is not the end goal. We wanted to create a community that invites people to come to experience being deeply known and loved, an experience so compelling that they become eager to go—to go free the prisoner, feed the hungry, comfort the grieving, love the addicted and mentally anguished, house the homeless and "stand in and close the gap" between those who have what they need to fulfill their God-given potential and those who do not.

After a few more discussions over coffee, Randall and I began hosting Explorers Groups for all who wanted to learn about the core commitments members of this new community would make. After sharing our vision with over a hundred explorers, nine founding members made a year-long commitment to New Creation Community on Easter of 2000. New Creation Community's call and core commitments—one of which is to allow ourself to be deeply known and loved in a small circle of loving accountability—helped lay the foundation from which Recovery Café's heart and guiding principles emerged.

2

HEARTS
BROKEN OPEN

To be a conscious person in this world, to be aware of all the suffering and the beauty, means to have your heart broken over and over again.

Sharon Salzberg

We've been given eyes to see, but the question becomes, do we let our hearts be broken by that reality, and then, do we act?

Dorothy Day

WHEN I agreed to move to Seattle, I thought I would end up doing something totally different from my work with homeless, mentally anguished and addicted individuals. At least that's what I thought until Billy Hart, a friend, godfather of our daughter Phoebe and a comic genius, came to Seattle for a visit. Before discovering Samaritan Inns and moving into Lazarus House, Billy had spent half of his life addicted to drugs and/or in federal prison. Samaritan Inns helped set him free and set his feet on solid ground.

During Billy's first visit to Seattle we walked all over downtown exploring the distinct neighborhoods. We inevitably kept running into people who were trapped in homelessness and addiction. Billy observed my response to each person we encountered. Finally he put his hand on my arm and said, "Who do you think you are kidding? You can still track an addict from ten miles away. This is the need that breaks your heart."

As someone seeking what I was supposed to do in the next phase of my life, I took Billy's observation very seriously. I began setting up appointments with leaders of existing non-profits all over Seattle, asking each one, "What need is not being met here?"

What became clear was that Seattle had several highly accomplished, low-income housing developers. There was no need for another low-income housing developer to create decent, affordable, drug and alcohol-free housing as Samaritan Inns had done in DC. There was and is need for many more units but not for more developers.

The need that emerged from my research was for on-going recovery support for women and men who suffered from homelessness, addiction and some other mental health challenge who were trying to attain and then maintain stability. Even those who were lucky enough to get into a 28-day or six month, in-patient treatment program found that on day 29, or the first day of month seven, they were on their own again, without daily support from community. Often women and men fortunate enough to move into beautiful, newly renovated, low-income housing discovered they could not maintain their recovery from addiction and co-occurring disorders and eventually landed back on the streets with one more failure under their belts.

Every week in New Creation Community's weekly gathering I shared what I was learning from other non-profits, and acknowledged that my heart continued to break for those traumatized by early childhood abuse, homelessness, addiction and other mental health challenges without any place to heal or to come to know themselves as loved.

One week, Ruby Takushi, a respected psychologist and university professor, in her gentle but resolute voice, responded, "Killian, that need breaks my heart, too." Before moving to Seattle, Ruby and her husband, Mark, had been members of the Church of the Saviour. Gordon had officiated their wedding. I thought of all the non-profits that had been birthed out of our DC faith community once a second person responded to the same need. I felt both excitement and the fear of being overwhelmed. I suspected we were in for a wild ride.

Ruby and I both continued to gather information regarding this need that broke our hearts and what was and was not being done in Seattle to address it. A year into our research an article was published in *Faith at Work* magazine about our own New Creation Community. Mary Crow, a dental hygienist living on Bainbridge Island, read the article. My phone number was not listed in the article, but eventually Mary tracked it down and called me at home.

Mary shared with me during that first phone call, "I have always dreamed of being a part of an intentional community committed to contemplation and action. In past years I even considered moving to DC just to become a part of the Church of the Saviour community." I told Mary the time and place of our weekly gathering and expressed how much we would love for her to come and explore. Just before hanging up the phone, I asked, "Mary, would you by any chance have an interest in being part of a response to the needs of homeless, mentally anguished, addicted women and men?" I sensed she was smiling on the other end of the phone as she responded, "Yes, and I have twenty years in recovery."

I hung up the phone feeling more energized than ever. We did not have a bank account, a 501(c)3 non-profit status, a building or a dime designated to our vision, which was just beginning to unfold. But Ruby, Mary and I soon understood that somehow we had been given the immense gift of each other.

Other members of New Creation Community joined Ruby, Mary and me in acting as an incubator for this developing call, including Theron Shaw, Angie Wolle, Cecilia McKean, Randall Mullins, LeAnne Moss, and others. Like gardeners watching for spring's earliest blooms, we gathered every Friday morning at 6:00 a.m.

to wait in silence, to pray for our next steps, "for the way to open," as Quakers say, and to share any findings from our research.

Gordon Cosby's warning to me in the early days of nurturing Samaritan Inns rang true in these early days of nurturing Recovery Café. He said, "Some people, out of their need for control, hold their call too tightly and risk smothering it to death. But your temptation is to give away your spiritual authority too quickly out of fear of being overwhelmed and out of a desire to be inclusive. When you give away the authority that comes with your call too quickly, the healing structure you are creating can lose its essence even before it is fully formed." I now understand his wisdom to mean, it is important for mothers to carry their babies full-term and then, slowly but surely "let go and trust."

At the Church of the Saviour we had an abundance of opportunities to observe the creation and sustaining of non-profit organizations. The church community was the fertile soil out of which over forty non-profits serving the poor have grown since its founding in 1947. We observed the various stages through which organizations move, beginning with their founding "myths" or truths so deep that they can't be directly defined, only "talked around" through stories. Those *myths,* or profound truths, which speak to us on a deeper than rational level, compel us to draw others into what we are envisioning and eventually evolve into a *movement.*

The movement may involve only a handful of people initially, but as the essence of the movement is fanned it enfolds a growing number of individuals who are touched by the founding truths. Movement to *machine*—or organizational structure that holds the essence and vision—requires an increasing variety of gifts.

As financial and human resources are drawn to and invested in the movement and the organizational structure effectively holds the essence of the vision, it is important that the structure remain nimble.

Organizations are living organisms that need to remain flexible enough to continuously evolve and grow. If the structure becomes too rigid, or calcified, the living organism and soul the structure holds may die. Many organizations move from the machine stage to *mausoleum* stage. Time and growth are two things that make an organization vulnerable to losing its essence. Over time, an indication that an organization's structure is becoming calcified is when the team becomes highly risk adverse and more concerned about their own job security than about the structure's capacity to respond effectively to the need it was created to address.

Just as we need to stay grounded in our spiritual practices, we need to stay rooted in our founding truths that keep our transformative vision alive.

Founding Myth→Movement→ Machine→ Met Needs

or

Founding Myth→ Movement→ Machine→ Mausoleum

. . .

So many played significant roles, directly and indirectly, in the development of Recovery Café. Charlotte Guyman and I met in September of 1999, when my daughter, Kietrie, and her daughter, Elizabeth, entered middle school together. Both of us had just left work that challenged us, consumed us and from which, to a large, sometimes not so healthy degree, we drew our identity. We connected immediately. Charlotte, who lives from a loving, wide-open heart, grew up in the Seattle area and has many deep friendships in Seattle. As a recent transplant from Washington, DC, I had not yet developed deep friendships in Seattle. Thanks to Charlotte's strong gift of connecting people and her generous, non-possessive understanding of friendship, I met deep-spirited and energizing Emmy Nielson. Emmy had lost her husband to cancer three months prior to our move to Seattle.

Emmy and I met weekly to run and talk. The loss of one's husband and a move across the country are not comparable, but Emmy and I both were grieving and both had been stripped of life as we had known it. We connected immediately and bypassed all surface chitchat. Most of our conversations were about the spiritual journey and what it required of us. But there was also lots of healing laughter. We both love to laugh. One Friday morning, following New Creation's 6:00 a.m. prayer gathering, I met Emmy for a run. At the end of that run, standing on Emmy's front porch, still sweating, I reported the latest in the unfolding vision for a healing center for Seattle's most vulnerable women and men. "Everyone needs a place to heal," I said.

Without any fanfare, Emmy responded, "I'd like to make a significant contribution towards the creation of this healing center." Emmy was the first person outside of New Creation Community to see the vision, to see the "not yet." She was the first to invest money in making our dream a reality. Emmy gave much more than money toward the dream of Recovery Café. As our friendship deepened, so did our shared commitment to the dream. Eventually, she would chair Recovery Café's Board of Directors and co-chair our capital campaign, teach in our School for Recovery, serve as a "bridge builder" (widening the circle of caring by inviting others) for every annual "Standing in the Gap" education of the heart/fundraiser event, and continue to invest her love and financial resources in the healing work of Recovery Café.

With Emmy's initial commitment in hand, we were able to go to landlords with more than just a dream. Even with the money to pay upfront rent for an entire, five-year lease, finding a landlord who would rent to us was an uphill slog. Place after place showed interest until we shared that our non-profit's dream was to welcome women and men who had suffered from "homelessness, addiction and other mental health challenges." Most landlords did not want to rent commercial space on the street level of their building to people they felt would be bad for the neighborhood businesses or for their tenants in the apartments above the commercial space. Although we pursued every lead, we could not find a landlord willing to rent to us in a neighborhood that was not plagued by the drug trade and hazardous for our future Members.

There was a space for rent on Fairview—the street that now runs through Amazon's Headquarters—that excited some of the New Creation Community members. Before we could go through the steps toward signing a lease for that space, Mary Crow had a dream that we had leased the space, invested in the necessary tenant improvements and then the space was bulldozed and developed by a for-profit developer. We were not sure if Mary's dream was guidance or just her subconscious processing fears of committing to that particular space or something totally unrelated. But, since New Creation Community members were praying for guidance and for each next step—while we followed up on every option—we interpreted Mary's dream as guidance and let the space go. A year later, an article on the front page of the *Seattle Times* revealed the commercial space in Mary's dream had been bought by a developer with plans to demolish the original structure and build a multi-storied condominium development.

Several members of New Creation Community continued to gather at 6:00 a.m. every Friday morning for centering/contemplative prayer and then to faithfully "turn over every stone" seeking guidance we trusted would be given at every step. That guidance came next in the form of Bill Hallerman, a visionary leader in the Archdiocesan Housing Authority.

As we chatted in line for lunch at an AHA retreat, he told me about a ground-level commercial space on 2nd and Bell in downtown Seattle. I skipped the lunch and afternoon session, drove straight to that address, peeked in the floor to ceiling windows and left Bill a voice message, "How soon can we talk about the terms of leasing this space?"

Six months and $150,000 in tenant improvements later, we welcomed our first Members to our beautiful, trendy, 1,700-square-foot "healing center in a Café setting" at the corner of 2nd and Bell. We called those who were ready to commit to three requirements "Members" because most had never been a member of anything in their entire lives and the term "Member" connotes belonging.

The membership requirements were:

1. To have twenty-four hours, drug and alcohol-free.

2. To meet weekly with a small, loving accountability group called a Recovery Circle.

3. To contribute by helping to maintain the physical space and to create a culture of healing and unconditional love.

During our three years at 2nd and Bell, Recovery Café held hundreds of men and women as they established a foundation in recovery on which they could build the rest of their lives.

3

WE BELONG TO EACH OTHER

I understand now that my welfare is only possible if I acknowledge my unity with all the people of the world without exception.

Leo Tolstoy

If we have no peace, it is because we have forgotten we belong to each other.

Mother Teresa

[In the community] we talk about how God has brought us together. I love to hear each one talking about where he or she was before coming to our community... and then there is a consciousness that now we are together. A few years ago we were dispersed; we did not know each other. Now we are together; we belong to each other. We realize what an incredible gift God has given us, to bring us together from different lands of pain and loneliness, and to become one people. We become more conscious that we are responsible for each other.

Jean Vanier

BOB was one of those early Members at 2nd and Bell. He had survived a childhood of neglect, like most of our Members. Out of a deep hunger for belonging, Bob joined a violent gang. He had tattoos all over his body advertising his "intimate" association with his gang. He proudly ran with this gang for fifteen years.

When Bob first found his way to Recovery Café, he was no longer proud. He was beaten nearly to death by meth and desperately wanted and needed help getting out of the deep pit he was in. Bob showed up at the Café every day for six months. He underwent the painful process of having his tattoos removed for fear he would be recognized by a member of his former gang and "punished" for defecting. Toward the end of six months, Bob pulled me aside and whispered, "I turned my gun over to the police this morning."

"What gun?" I asked, nervously.

"The one I have had strapped to my leg every day for the past six months," he confessed.

He went on to explain, "I'm beginning to understand that true security doesn't come from having a gun. It comes from within."

As a Member of Recovery Café and New Creation Community, Bob began to understand what it means to love and receive love and to belong to a people. After a year of working hard to establish a foundation in recovery, Bob wanted to return to Michigan to make amends to the kids he had abandoned for a life of drugs and violence. He was blown away when New Creation Community bought him a bus ticket to go there for Christmas.

Bob knew making amends to his two children, who were almost adults, would not be easy. He had no idea it would go as poorly as it did. His kids didn't want to have anything to do with him. Devastated, Bob returned to Seattle, found a dealer and got loaded. But all that work he had done on his recovery was not lost.

His previous foundation in recovery called to him in between each attempt to forget his failure to reconcile with his biological family by getting high.

A couple of weeks passed before the call to recovery was more compelling than the need to numb his pain and Bob returned to the Café. No one knows why it takes some individuals three or four runs to really get recovery and others never do. It is mystery. Bob truly humbled himself and started the work all over again of building a foundation on which he could grow for the rest of his life. This time he completely immersed himself in community, worked the 12-steps, and dug up and dealt with childhood trauma with the help of a therapist.

Eventually, with a gift from New Creation Community, Bob purchased new tools and returned to construction work, and he ultimately started his own construction company. Eight years later, surrounded by a community of true friends, Bob married Joan in a beautiful wedding, at sunset, on one of the San Juan

Islands. Understandably emotional on his wedding day, Bob told me moments before the ceremony, "I would not be getting married today if Recovery Café had not saved my life."

Today, Bob's daughter, son-in-law and their baby are living in Seattle because they want to be near Bob and Joan. Bob stops by the Café occasionally to say, "Thank you for saving my life." Truth is, he and others like him are saving mine through their deep authenticity and great love.

• • •

A favorite story of mine is about the woman caught in the act of adultery and brought by the religious authorities to Jesus.

The religious authorities, seeking to trick Jesus into a wrong answer, ask, "According to Mosaic law, this woman should be stoned to death; what do you say?"

Jesus did not respond immediately, but kneeled and

began writing in the dirt with his finger. Perhaps he needed time to connect with his deepest, truest self instead of making an automatic response.

Perhaps, as St. Augustine suggests, writing with his finger was Jesus' way of alluding to the story of the ten commandments being written by God's finger on stone—one of which was "thou shall not kill"—and Jesus' way of claiming his authority as "justice manifest."

Perhaps Jesus sensed the rising energy of the crowd and understood that we are capable of worse things when caught up in a mob than when we are able to pause and connect with our own, truest self.

What we know from the story is that Jesus called them to self-reflection, not as a mob, but as individuals. He said, "Let the ONE who has not sinned be the ONE to cast the first stone."

The mob diffused, individuals slipped away, one by one, leaving Jesus alone with the traumatized woman.

When he spoke to her she opened her eyes and saw that no one but Jesus remained. Jesus asked, "Where are your accusers? Does no one condemn you?" She must have been too stunned to answer, so Jesus continued, "Neither do I condemn you." And then he challenged her to stop the behaviors that create suffering for herself and others saying, "Go and sin no more."

We all need opportunities to grow through our mistakes. This story, like Bob's story, reminds me that we are unconditionally loved just as we are, and that we are so much more than our worst act. We are continuously invited to let go of behaviors that are not consistent with our truest self and, therefore, do not free us to live life to the absolute fullest, manifesting love in all we say and do.

•　•　•

We used every square inch of our 2nd and Bell space, but eventually we could not respond to the increasing need in that amount of space. Recovery Café was growing and we were in need of a permanent home. Members were longing for more tools to help them deepen and grow. The vision for our School for Recovery was given, and since then has grown to offer classes in Centering Prayer, Meditation, Spiritual Growth, Communication, Resumé Writing, Creative Writing, Anger Management, Grieving Our Losses, Transforming Trauma, Nutrition, Chi Gong, Yoga, Healing through the Arts, The Inward Outward Journey, Relapse Prevention, the 12-steps and the list goes on and on.

To create a place of true belonging, our commitment was and has always been to meet people where they are. Part of meeting people where they are means never pushing religious beliefs on others. To push others, especially when they are quite vulnerable, to adopt a particular faith perspective can be a form of violence to their spirit. The School for Recovery classes give everyone tools to dig deep within ourselves where we may discover that the treasure buried underneath the layers of hurt is unconditional love. If we are created in the image of God, and God is love, than that place of unconditional love is not just in some of us, it is in all of us. Whether we are Christian, Buddhist, Muslim, Hindu, Jewish or not affiliated with any faith tradition at all; whether we have made egregious mistakes and experienced epic failure or are at the "top of our game;" whether we are consumed by grief or alive with joy, there is what Martin Luther King, Jr. called "love-force" at the core of our being.

Hanging on the Café's walls are our "cloud of witnesses" who embody/embodied that same "love-force" we are unearthing in ourselves. There are beautiful, framed photos of Rosa Parks, Sojourner Truth, Cesar Chavez, Nelson Mandela, Martin Luther King, Jr., Mahatma Gandhi, the Dalai Lama, Mother Teresa, and Chief Seattle.

Just outside at street level is an engaging sculpture of the "Servant Christ" kneeling to wash feet, a special gift given anonymously to Recovery Café. The plaque on the statue reads: "Recovery Café is a supportive community which welcomes women and men from all backgrounds and spiritual traditions. Sculptor Jimilu Mason's 'Servant Christ' represents the humility, loving kindness and service which is at the heart of Recovery Café."

Many people passing by stop to interact with the "Servant Christ." Some place gifts in his rugged, outstretched hands. Some of the offerings we've discovered in his hands include various pieces of fruit, flowers, colorful fall leaves, coins, a feather, a blunt, a bar of soap, a Budweiser, a boiled egg, a polished pebble, a Narcotics Anonymous ten-month coin, and once someone placed a handsome, red beret upon his head.

•   •   •

Looking back, during the time we were searching for the first space for Recovery Café's welcoming, healing work to begin, Charlotte was introducing me to more of her friends. I would meet them for walks or runs. Everyone I met eventually wanted to talk about the spiritual life. After the third friend of Charlotte's shared her spiritual hunger with me, I suggested to Charlotte that we form a "spiritual growth" group in which we could all grow together and learn from each other. Not only is community the soil in which spiritual transformation takes place, but the cartilage in my knees was almost gone from a lifetime of running and I didn't think I could meet anyone else for a weekly run.

That's how "Swadyayees" was born. The group was named after a movement in India that encouraged those who had been freed from lives of demoralizing poverty to return to their villages and accompany others seeking to escape that fate. Accompanying others was the heart of this Indian movement.

Initially the nine "Swads" made three simple commitments. We would show up for our regular gatherings, making them a practical priority in our busy lives. We would come prepared, having read the agreed upon book—chosen to challenge us and nurture spiritual growth—and we would allow ourselves to be deeply known, sharing our struggles as well as our joys. During our very first gathering there was an earthquake in Seattle measuring 6.8 in magnitude. Gordon Cosby often described the spiritual life as a series of inner landslides and inner earthquakes so I saw this earthquake as a very good omen. Fifteen years later, the Swads still meet regularly.

In almost every regular meeting in the Swad gatherings, my sharing touched on my deepening sense of call to create a healing community for some of Seattle's most vulnerable. I would describe Recovery Cafè to the limit of my vision. At the beginning of one of our silent retreats, I shared how painful it was to carry this "baby" so long past its due date. Our 2nd and Bell location had let us begin, but we desperately needed more space to respond to those still suffering. During the silence one of the Swads handed me a note, which said, "I want to help you attain a permanent home for this healing community."

A week later, after our morning run, I followed up with

her, asking her for the first gift to begin the campaign which would result in the purchase of an old building that had been greatly reduced due to the 2008 recession. Judging from the surprise on her face, I must have suggested an amount higher than what she was thinking when she slipped me the note during the silent retreat. She readjusted her thinking. The next week when we met to run, she shared, enthusiastically, "We will do it."

Once, after receiving an extravagant gift from this same couple, another friend emoted, "We will never be able to repay you for your generosity." With his boyish grin, the husband in this duo quipped, "You are right. You will never be able to repay us."

With this significant commitment in hand—which we will never be able to repay—I invited other Swads, and everyone I knew, to invest in purchasing, gutting, and renovating the building to meet our specific program needs. Many gave so generously we were often moved to tears. I was particularly touched by one woman whose annual budget allowed her to make a generous gift of $100, but she wanted to give $1,000. So she pledged $100 per year for ten years.

Following this silent part of our capital campaign, our board announced our goal of $12.7 million dollars. Before its conclusion we had asked everyone in Seattle to contribute, or so it felt. Maureen Lee, a great lover of people and natural connector who grew up in Seattle, joined forces with Emmy in leading this campaign. Between the two of them and other Recovery Café board members, like the witty, large-hearted and pragmatic Rod Bench, we pursued every possible opportunity in search of capital gifts.

As this capital campaign gathered energy, incomparably smart and multi-talented Stephanie Jones, our Finance Director, who had led the pursuit and purchase of the building, turned her energies toward directing the renovation. She helped attain complex New Market Tax Credits, which ultimately contributed a million dollars toward the dream becoming a reality.

A couple of years after the first Swad meeting, Emmy and I decided to respond to the spiritual hunger we recognized everywhere and in almost everyone by starting a few similar groups. These groups gathered around the same clear commitments the Swads initially gathered around; however, we added a fourth commitment for these new groups: "I will spend a specific amount of time each day in silence, in some contemplative practice." Simone Weil, the French philosopher, wrote: "If we go down into ourselves, we find that we possess exactly what we desire."

Emmy and I decided unless participants in these groups were willing at least to begin a contemplative practice, all the spiritual books in the world and warm experiences of community were not going to be very fruitful. I reflected on the parable of the seed that fell on good soil in Matthew 13. The plants grew, but the weeds soon choked the plants to death. We felt no matter how hard we worked to create soil nutritious enough to produce spiritual growth, if seekers did not begin to put down deep, spiritual roots through a contemplative practice, the cares and busy-ness of their lives, the weeds, would choke to death any growth they might experience.

Eventually, there were seven spiritual growth groups gathering around beginning, clear commitments. The leadership and facilitation were shared. It concerned me though that these groups might be more about the participants' desire for self-actualization, for becoming the best, most polished persons we could become for our own sake and the sake of those in our own close circle of family and friends.

We needed to stay conscious that planting ourselves in the soil of community and showing up daily through meditation or contemplative prayer as a means of surrendering our lives, was not just about our own self-actualization, but was for the sake of a wounded world desperately in need of healing and justice. That healing and justice can flow through us, but is not from us and is certainly not "about" us.

The Sufi tell a story about a spiritual seeker who was distracted by the sick, crippled and beaten down who continuously passed by as he tried to pray. Finally he cried, "Great God, how is it that a loving creator can see such things and do nothing about them?"

Out of the long silence, God said, "I did do something about them. I made you."

We sought to connect the members of these spiritual growth groups with Members of Recovery Café in every way we could imagine, even suggesting that we add a commitment to nurture relationships that cross racial, economic and religious boundaries—which is one of New Creation Community's original commitments. Most of the members of the spiritual growth groups had volunteered in non-profits and given generously to organizations serving the poor. Most had not developed authentic relationships with individuals who were poor.

Elizabeth O'Connor said it well in her book, *The New Community*: "The real problem with the structures of the Church is that they do not often allow us to become engaged in the anguish of people whose needs, and accents, and ways are different from our own. They do not allow us to feel. It was not enough for Moses to see the misery of a slave people. He had to identify with them—to be able to say 'my people.'"

As Recovery Café celebrates its eleventh year, most members of these spiritual growth groups, along with other congregations like St. Joe's, University Presbyterian, Japanese Presbyterian, Plymouth Church and University Congregational Church and others are bridge builders for our annual "Standing in the Gap" event. They serve as volunteer board members, teach in the School for Recovery, listen deeply as ministers of presence, educate others as activists and advocates, walk with Recovery Café's walking club, cook dinner at Open Mic nights, bake cakes for Members' birthdays, make themselves vulnerable as resource raisers and seek deepening relationships with the women and men who find their way from the streets to Recovery Café. Two streams, once parallel, are merging and flowing from and into an ocean of unconditional love.

These streams are flowing beyond Seattle. We have walked closely with a group of faithful friends who now operate Recovery Café San José, and another group of friends who operate Everett Recovery Café in Everett, Washington. We are currently supporting a group in Spokane and several other groups in Washington State and as far away as New Hampshire as they seek to replicate Recovery Café's model. Hoping to share it in the most helpful ways possible keeps us reflecting on: *"What makes Recovery Café? What is our special sauce?"*

4

RADICAL
HOSPITALITY

Hospitality is not to change people, but to offer them space where change can take place. It is not to bring men and women over to our side, but to offer freedom undisturbed by dividing lines… The paradox of hospitality is that it wants to create emptiness; not a fearful emptiness, but a friendly emptiness where strangers can enter and discover themselves as created free; free to sing their own songs, speak their own languages, dance their own dances; free also to leave and follow their own vocations. Hospitality is not a subtle invitation to adopt the lifestyle of the host, but the gift of a chance for the guest to find their own.

Henri J.M. Nouwen

OUR mission is to welcome women and men who have suffered homelessness, addiction and other mental health challenges into a community where they come to know they are loved and that they have gifts to share.

If individuals are to establish a foundation in recovery that they can build on for the rest of their lives they will need on-going support in the context of a healing, recovery community. Isolation is the nemesis of early recovery.

Individuals in early recovery are told to disassociate from people, places and things that are part of their "using" past. However, breaking from destructive relationships, they end up isolated and equally vulnerable to relapse. We all need to replace destructive relationships associated with our addiction/mental health challenge with positive relationships supportive of our recovery. That's why the Recovery Café model, or some form of on-going, supportive recovery community, is needed in every county and state.

Our community understands that recovery from mental health challenges and from addiction are two sides of the same coin. Because mental health and addiction funding streams are kept separate, their treatments also have been kept separate. Recovery Café addresses recovery from addiction and other mental health challenges under the same roof.

Constant attention must be given to creating and maintaining a culture that is healing, inclusive, respectful of all members of the community, diverse, and economically sustainable. Key to creating a healing culture—and part of our special sauce—is to hire staff who believe in the vision and are passionate about the mission. Even if the staff member's role is technology or finance and not program related, it is important that everyone on the team help hold the vision and maintain the culture. We have a weekly meeting for staff members for the sole purpose of deepening relationships, which nurtures a team spirit among the staff. This deep connection helps us give each other the benefit of the doubt—trusting that each of us is doing our very best—especially when we are making judgment calls under stress.

Unlike work cultures where competition drives individuals to present only a polished image of themselves, in the Friday staff meeting Recovery Café's teammates share the places where we struggle and are vulnerable. We attempt to do with each other what we ask the Members to do in their Recovery Circles, to allow ourselves to be deeply known and loved.

Ultimately, the vision and mission must be internalized by staff, Members, volunteers and donors, as well. The deeper the vision and mission are internalized by all those who participate in any way in the community, the stronger the healing culture will be. Our Jesuit Volunteer Corps Northwest year-long volunteers and interns bring fresh energy and passion. Every person brings a piece to the creation and maintenance of a healing, recovery culture/community. No one person can or needs to bring all the gifts. Everyone brings their unique gifts to the whole.

Early on, Recovery Café invited all Members to participate in the creation of guiding principles, which would support the vision and mission. Those guiding principles are:

> To live prayerfully (i.e. with reverence for all)
> To practice compassion
> To show respect
> To give and forgive
> To encourage growth

These guiding principles are critical to fostering the culture of healing and are verbally reinforced before the entire Recovery Café community every day at the time that everyone—staff, Members, volunteers, and interns—gathers for five minutes of silence. After the silence we recognize those Members of the community who went the extra mile in service to make our community run smoothly and we recognize two or three Members of the community who were "caught in the act" of building our culture of kindness.

Many Members are visibly uncomfortable the first few times they are thanked in our daily gathering and all eyes are on them. But over time, as they come to believe that they truly are kind and they really are community builders, their discomfort fades and they even seem to enjoy the affirmation.

An ingredient in our special sauce is staying anchored in powerful guiding principles instead of a suffocating number of rules. It is better to have strong guiding principles than to create so many rules that staff and Members cannot possibly remember them or follow them all. Of course, some rules are needed in any community for they express how the guiding principles are lived out in specific actions and behaviors. They provide some structure. But it is possible to have so many rules that community members feel we are walking on eggshells. In a healing community/culture there must be room to make mistakes and for mistakes to become learning experiences.

• • •

When a suffering individual first walks in the door of Recovery Café, she or he is warmly greeted by one of our dedicated managers, like kind, tenderhearted Teresa Perillo, or warm and embracing Nancy Batayola. If he or she is not currently on a mood-altering substance, an invitation is extended to become our "guest for the day." One "guest for the day" was Tiffany Turner, who became a Member, and then after building a foundation in recovery, began training to become an addictions counselor. She is now part of Recovery Café's staff, and is an instrument of the same unconditional love that transformed her life.

Each new guest is invited to participate in all the day's activities such as our practice of five minutes of silence before lunch, an introduction to the community during announcements, the daily affirmation of our guiding principles, nutritious meals, the experience of caring and loving community and Latte Hour. Latte Hour is the time each afternoon during which Recovery Café Members who have completed our barista training practice their new skills preparing made-to-order, espresso drinks for community Members.

When Starbucks first donated the "Cadillac" espresso machine that they had replaced in their stores with faster, automatic models, one member of our board questioned the importance of an espresso machine in a community serving needs that are more basic according to Maslow's hierarchy of needs. It was an opportunity to reaffirm the essence of our mission and to help all of us internalize that essence at deeper levels.

The most basic need of every human being is to love and receive love. Nine out of ten Recovery Café Members have experienced childhood trauma, and many have suffered one trauma after another since childhood. Most Recovery Café Members have received so much less love than they needed throughout their lives that anything we can possibly do to communicate unconditional love is critical. For individuals who are not welcome in all places and cannot afford a special coffee drink even in places where they might be welcome, receiving a drink made especially for them, exactly as they requested, contributes toward meeting that most basic need to know that they are loved and that their lives matter.

When the warm and delightful then-president of Starbucks, Jim Donald, visited Recovery Café, I explained to him that handing someone a hot drink made especially for her or him is a form of "communion." Taking it a step too far, I added, "It's like saying, 'this is the Latte of Christ, prepared especially for you.'" Not offended in the least, Jim joked, "Latte of Christ! I can see it now on our menus and in our next advertising campaign."

If the guest chooses, she or he can become a Member of Recovery Café and an orientation to our community is scheduled. The three primary commitments required of Members are the same as when we began on 2nd and Bell:

First: Members must be drug and alcohol-free for the twenty-four hours prior to showing up at Recovery Café.

Many of our Members are seeking to put together hours, days, weeks, months and years of recovery time. Whether they are living on the streets, in shelters or in low-income housing buildings, almost everywhere they go they are surrounded by people using drugs and/or alcohol and the behaviors that accompany drug use. In order for Recovery Café to be a true refuge it is important that it be a drug and alcohol-free environment.

Second: Members must commit to participating in a weekly Recovery Circle, a loving accountability group.

There are currently forty-two Recovery Circles, meeting at different times throughout the week. Over half of these Recovery Circles are led by Recovery Café

Members, who receive weekly training for and support in this significant leadership role. Recovery Circles are the heart of the Recovery Café. They are the place where women and men slowly begin to trust again and allow themselves to be known and loved. Allowing ourselves to be deeply known is the most effective form of accountability. When others know us from having listened to our weekly sharing for months or years, they can recognize mental, physical and spiritual health indicators we may not see in ourselves and recognize habitual, destructive behavior patterns we may be blind to in ourselves.

There is a power in being both known and loved, at the same time, and this is part of Recovery Café's special sauce. Many of our Members have never before experienced the unconditional love that they experience in their Recovery Circles and the larger Recovery Café community. Many have never before been able to bring to speech their past traumas and the resulting, destructive behaviors and have those "secrets" met and held by unconditional love.

The year before coming to Recovery Café Lucy was taken to the emergency room and hospitalized nine times in mental health crises. During the nine years she participated in her weekly Recovery Circle she was hospitalized only once. Her circle-mates knew her well enough and loved her deeply enough to help her manage her mental health symptoms so they did not escalate to the point of landing her in the emergency room. For example, when the tormenting voices grew too much to bear her circle-mates would remind her that "the voices are always worse when your plate is too full." They would discuss ways she might reduce her stress while still accomplishing her goals. During those nine years she completed her Bachelor of Arts degree and remained stable in her housing. She now has a network of supportive friends outside Recovery Café, but checks in regularly to say hello and let us know all is well.

Dave Shull, Dean of the School for Recovery, supervisor of all our interns from graduate schools and counseling degree programs, and one of the trainers of our Recovery Circle Facilitators, brings profound, healing presence and laughter to our staff, volunteers and Members. He also leads one of the Recovery Circles. During one of his circles a Member shared that he had been bullied throughout his childhood and recalled all the hurtful names he'd been called. Another Member of the group, when it was her turn, offered her valuable experience as a gift to this circle-mate. "I was called many derogatory names, as well. Now I know my name is 'beloved.' I refuse to listen to any other name."

When William received some bad news, he took off and got loaded. Typically when someone relapses it may take weeks or months for them to find their way back to recovery and stability. William was sitting on the front step the very next day. I asked him what accounted for his being able to return from relapse so quickly. He replied, "This is the first time anyone cared whether I returned or not."

Circle attendance is tracked through a specially

designed software program. We all need to be held to the practices that help us become who we say we want to become. The act of keeping attendance helps everyone show up for our circle on days when showing up feels like the last thing we want to do.

Third: Members commit to being contributors, which means participating in the daily upkeep of the facility and daily operations of the Café and helping hold the sacred, healing space needed by all in the Café community.

Community Members are expected to sign up for a chore each day, such as preparing food in the kitchen (which requires attaining a food handler's permit), taking out garbage, re-stocking food supplies, cleaning the coffee bar, wiping down tables, mopping, vacuuming, and cleaning the restrooms. Caring for the physical space instills a sense of ownership of and responsibility for the community and contributing helps build self-esteem. That sense of being a contributor deepens as Members participate in each other's healing in Recovery Circles, classes and daily interactions around the tables.

• • •

The suffering individual usually arrives at Recovery Café beaten down by addiction, mental illness and life on the streets. Their shame is so heavy that most have trouble lifting their heads and looking anyone in the eyes. What they don't fully understand at this early stage of recovery is that their showing up and their awareness of their profound need for healing is a crucial part of the healing process.

Many of our staff, volunteers and donors walk through the same front door as our Members, but are much less aware of our need for others to be invited into our brokenness and most stubborn struggles. Many come to meet our shared human need to serve, and somewhere along the way discover our own need for healing. Through the process of showing up and listening to Members share their stories with startling honesty and authenticity, staff, volunteers and donors begin to understand that at the center of every addiction and obsessive behavior there is a wound. There is pain. The wound may not be as deep or as excruciating for some as for others, but it is there.

We begin to understand that wound is there in the obsessive gambler, the internet porn addict, the compulsive shopper, the "control freak," the compulsive overeater, and even, the workaholic. I know that wound is there in me. For many years I used food to numb the ache of depression. That caused me to check out mentally and emotionally, when what was most needed was for me to pay close attention, to be fully present.

In Tibetan Buddhism, the hungry ghost is a metaphor for one of the conditions of life. Hungry ghosts are depicted with enormous, empty stomachs and tiny necks. They want to eat to fill their emptiness, but are not equipped to swallow. Gabor Maté explains, "The hungry ghosts are tortured by not being able to fill their emptiness, and tortured even more by becoming addicted to those things they, mistakenly, think will bring relief."

Søren Kierkegaard, the nineteenth century Danish philosopher and author, wrote: "We tranquilize ourselves with the trivial to avoid confronting the truth about our own darkness."

How can we hope to respond to the challenges of our times when we are tranquilizing ourselves, day in and day out, with the trivial, with things that have no eternal value, no power to heal or create a more just world?

In our community everyone involved comes to know that we are all recovering from something and in need of the power of authentic, honest, healing community. One major donor admitted, "I am not addicted to money itself, but to distributing it perfectly where it can make the most impact and be the most scalable. That addiction to perfection, control and to quantifiable results can be paralyzing and can rob me of the joy of giving. It often gets in the way of the good my resources can make possible."

Another volunteer described her need for recovery from her addiction/attachment to being "good." She shared: "My need to be so good makes me beat myself up when I make mistakes and makes me take myself way too seriously. It robs me of the joy of living."

"All this preoccupation with your own imperfection is not humility," wrote Evelyn Underhill, "but an insidious form of spiritual pride. And what do you expect to be? A saint? There are desperately few of them. And even they found that faults, which are the raw material of sanctity remember, take a desperate lot of working up."

We call our regular volunteers who come once a week to simply sit and listen "ministers of presence." One minister of presence, Mary Ann, was married to an alcoholic for many years. She shared:

> *I don't even know when I first knew that he was drinking too much because he drank at home; he didn't stay out*

somewhere. He didn't cause any real problems . . . he'd fall asleep. But it got to the point where I couldn't stand hearing the ice cubes when he got home. He'd open the refrigerator, and I'd be thinking, "Oh, here we go again." It was more that he fell asleep. He wasn't present. And I had a lot of kids! So did he. I kept saying, "Why are you doing this? Why?" And he would say, "I don't know. I don't know."

Jean Vanier, founder of the healing L'Arche communities, writes, "What is this 'essential' of our communities? Presence: being fully present to people who are fragile; being present to one another. To live fully the present moment and not to try to hide behind some past ideals or future utopia. Our human hearts are thirsting for presence: the presence of a friend; the presence of someone who will listen faithfully, who does not judge but who understands, appreciates, and through love lowers the barriers of inner fear and anguish. This presence implies compassion and tenderness as well as competence."

Most of us struggle with simply being present. Some

of us "check out" because we have not confronted our own pain and therefore cannot be present to the pain or demands of others. Others of us are so conditioned to think it is what we do and accomplish that counts that we've never developed a practice of simply being present.

So, another ingredient in the special sauce of Recovery Café is that almost everyone involved at any level and in any way knows that we are all both addicts and healers, both recipients and contributors, both those who welcome others into our community of belonging and those needing to be reminded daily that we ourselves are welcome. We all need to know we belong.

Mary Crow recalled an early moment that reinforced for her the significance of the gift of presence. "Zoe Strum was volunteering as a minister of presence for the first time, listening to a young man and asking him what movies he liked. Sounds normal doesn't it? Later, I found her in the office crying and asked what was wrong. This young man had told Zoe, 'no one sees me,' and shared it was the first time in his life someone took enough interest in him to listen to what he had to say."

Sometimes we are astonished when we learn that although we did not actually "do" anything for a certain individual, our simply being present or showing up allowed something to shift in his or her inner landscape that made space for deeper healing. Sometimes we discover that in simply being present to another's pain we experience the Divine in them that awakens the Divine in ourselves.

We cannot fix ourselves or anyone else. We can only choose to show up or be present to our own lives and the lives of others. We all have to discover practices that help us stay present to our lives and others and return to presence when we become aware of our disengagement or dissociation.

• • •

Recovery Café's special sauce includes a commitment

to excellence and beauty. There is an assumption among many who have always had what they need that the poor do not need beauty and excellence; that the "desperate" should feel lucky to get anything at all. This notion, if taken to an extreme, results in donations of soiled garments, broken toys and furniture with filthy, ripped upholstery.

Visitors are almost always surprised by the beauty of Recovery Café and its standard of excellence. One woman exclaimed, "I had no idea this place would be so beautiful. It's like the Fairmont," one of Seattle's finest hotels.

Our philosophy—which was shaped in part by Mary Cosby, married to Gordon—is that every single expression at Recovery Café must communicate love. That philosophy drives our commitment to preparing nutritious meals—often under the guidance of humble, gentle Brian Kosewski—and serving the food on brightly colored Fiesta Ware. That philosophy drives the exquisite interior design of our space. Laura

Donald, Lucia Baratta and Laurie Oki—three beautiful women, inside and out—are responsible for the vibrant color choices for our walls, carpet and upholstery. Those choices matter because they help us communicate "your life matters." For those who have suffered in body, mind and spirit, beauty is a healing salve. For those weary from trying to navigate the journey from chaos to stability, best practices which affirm the dignity and worth of every community Member are crucial. Those who have suffered the degradation of homelessness may not expect beauty and excellence, but they are the ones who especially need beauty and excellence.

When we were making tenant improvements to our first space at 2nd and Bell we ordered carpet tiles which would compliment the beautiful paint we had chosen for our walls and camouflage the inevitable coffee stains to come. The construction company mistakenly sent the wrong carpet tiles. The crew laying the tiles must have thought we had really bad taste, but they laid the tiles that were sent.

When I arrived the next day, excited to see the space with the carefully chosen carpet, I felt sick to my stomach. The carpet tiles that had been laid throughout the otherwise chic and colorful Cafè, were alternating zebra stripes that made me dizzy if I stared at the floor too long. I wondered if we could get used to the vertigo inducing zebra stripes, like getting used to a bad haircut, but there was just no way. We called the carpet supplier. When he saw the space he offered to give us the zebra carpet for free. We were grateful for his offer, but respectfully insisted that he remove the zebra tiles and install the pattern we had selected.

"Do you really think the women and men who come to your Recovery Café are going to care if the carpet is not a good match?" he asked.

"Honestly," we answered, "they probably won't care, because they are used to being treated as if their lives are somehow less valuable than the lives of others. But at Recovery Café, everything will communicate, 'you are loved and your life matters.'"

Johann Wolfgang von Goethe wrote, "The way you see people is the way you treat them and the way you treat them is what they become."

Anthony De Mello, one of my favorite spiritual teachers, tells this story:

"A man found an eagle's egg and put it in a nest of a barnyard hen. The eaglet hatched with the brood of chicks and grew up with them.

All his life the eagle did what the barnyard chicks did, thinking he was a barnyard chicken. He scratched the earth for worms and insects. He clucked and cackled. And he would thrash his wings and fly a few feet into the air.

Years passed and the eagle grew very old. One day he saw a magnificent bird above him in the cloudless sky. It glided in graceful majesty among the powerful wind currents, with scarcely a beat of its strong golden wings.

The old eagle looked up in awe. 'Who's that?' he asked.

'That's the eagle, the king of the birds,' said his neighbor. 'He belongs to the sky. We belong to the earth–we're chickens.' So the eagle lived and died a chicken, for that's what he thought he was."

Determined that our future members would come to know that they are "eagles, not chickens," the correct carpet was ordered and installed within two weeks. In the meantime, we had to live with the zebra tiles. Lots of jokes were made among our team during those two weeks about changing our name from Recovery Café to "Zebra Bar and Lounge."

•   •   •

Recovery Café's special sauce of radical hospitality includes feathered and furry, four-legged friends.

In the State of Washington everyone with a mental health diagnosis is allowed to certify their pet as a "companion animal." The pet is not required to go through rigorous training like noble, obedient, seeing-eye dogs. In fact, the companion animal does not have to be well-behaved at all. Since nine out of ten of our Members are in recovery from addiction and/or some other mental health challenge, ninety percent of our Members are allowed, by law, to bring their companion animals into restaurants and other public spaces. So Recovery Café's radical hospitality, by law, must include an assortment of sometimes ill-behaved companion animals who bring a sense of security and emotional well-being to their owners and sometimes a circus-like quality to our Café. Our Café community has included a cat named Cleopatra, a parrot named Boy George, a crow named Raven, whose owner taught him to flush the toilet, and even a hissing possum named Ophelia. In spite of the companion animal law, Ophelia and Raven were respectfully asked to remain outside the Café.

One early evening, just before dinner, a first-time guest, Raymond, walked through the door. I watched as Darren Kilian, one of our managers who is caring and self-reflective, approached Raymond, who was wearing a mid-length leather coat over his rotund stomach. Many late-stage alcoholics have extended, bloated stomachs related to liver disease.

Darren, warm and wise, as always, welcomed Raymond and inquired, "What kind of companion animal do you have?"

"What makes you think I have a companion animal?" Raymond replied, a bit defensively. At precisely that same moment, Darren, Raymond and I looked down at the long tail, hanging about six inches lower than Raymond's leather jacket, wagging back and forth like the pendulum of a grandfather clock. We all burst into laughter.

Then Raymond tentatively freed Buster, a light gray, forty-five-pound pit bull, from the confines of his leather jacket.

5

MUTUALLY
LIBERATING
RELATIONSHIPS

This is the true joy of life, the being used for a purpose recognized by yourself as a mighty one; being a force of nature instead of a feverish, selfish little clod of ailments and grievances, complaining that the world will not devote itself to making you happy.

I am of the opinion that my life belongs to the community, and as long as I live, it is my privilege to do for it whatever I can. I want to be thoroughly used up when I die, for the harder I work, the more I live. I rejoice in life for its own sake. Life is no 'brief candle' to me. It is a sort of splendid torch which I have got hold of for a moment, and I want to make it burn as brightly as possible before handing it on to future generations.

George Bernard Shaw

ANOTHER ingredient in the special sauce of Recovery Café is the opportunity for the homeless and those we call, for lack of a better name, the "home-blessed," to develop relationships with each other. Relationships, real relationships that cross barriers between individuals from different socio-economic realities, races, faith traditions, genders and sexual orientations are what change us.

The crossing of these barriers is not always smooth. Around the tables, over coffee, the messy work of reconciliation and community building is taking place on many different levels, every day.

It's important first to come to know someone as a human being, as a person who embodies both a "shadow side" and the "light of Divine Love," just like us, before diving into the issues that can be divisive.

Around the tables of Recovery Café, while sipping a latte, individuals can begin to hear each other's stories, discover commonalities, laugh and even cry together, and eventually stumble into addressing deep-seated biases that were taken in "with our mother's milk."

One individual of unusual wealth had served on the board of Recovery Café for years and intellectually understood the issues around homelessness, addiction and mental illness in the United States. We invited her to participate in a forty-hour, week-long training of Recovery Café Members who serve as facilitators of Recovery Circles. Sitting around the tables during that week of training with Recovery Café Members as they shared parts of their past and current realities blew down any remaining defenses of this faithful friend of Recovery Café. At the end of the week she shared, "I was completely unaware of how effectively I sweep the realities of the suffering poor under the rug and go about my life as if they do not exist, and I am one of Recovery Café's biggest fans."

Jonathan served three tours of duty in Afghanistan, suffered with PTSD, used alcohol to self-medicate the violent nightmares and now has three years of sustained recovery and Recovery Café membership. He shared: "One of my closest friends is Gerald. He's one of the funniest guys I've ever met and the best friend you could ever have. I never had a gay friend before coming to Recovery Café." The 14th Dalai Lama has written: "Every change of mind is first of all a change of heart."

All the articles, editorials, impassioned speeches, photographs and documentaries cannot touch that place within us where we know we are all one in the way that one authentic, mutually liberating relationship can. We deny the oneness of the human family at our own peril, at the risk of losing our own souls.

• • •

Fundraising for Recovery Café is based on the truth that generosity brings joy and deepens community.

We view fundraising as calling a widening circle of friends into deepening awareness of the oneness of the human family. Instead of an annual fundraising event where we invite people simply to make a donation to Recovery Café, our annual event is an invitation to become part of a movement by "standing in the gap" between those who have what they need to fulfill their God-given potential and those who do not. Of course, we ask for financial support at our "standing in the gap" event, which is brilliantly orchestrated by deeply grounded David Uhl, our Resource Development Director, along with our creative and comical office manager, Jeff King, and gentle, rock-solid-with-integrity Finance Director, Skye Stuart.

More importantly, we challenge ourselves and those who attend to "put our weight down" with some group of men and women who suffer exclusion and do not have what they need in the way of education, housing, health care and community which would make possible their becoming all they were created to become. Six friends of Recovery Café who exemplify "putting your weight down" are Michael King, Janet Holdcroft, Diane Tomhave, Maureen Lee, Vicki Allen and Mary Ellen Weber, all of whom invested money, time, energy and love into this community and who said, each in their own way, "I have received far more than I have given."

When we put our weight down with one group of suffering individuals—such as the homeless, mentally ill and addicted—that action connects us with all the suffering individuals across the globe. Likewise, putting our weight down with one expression of healing and hope—like Recovery Café—connects us with a worldwide movement of healing and hope.

Recovery Café's philosophy of fundraising can be traced back to Gordon Cosby's philosophy and practice of fundraising for over eighty years. When Gordon and Mary's foster son was sentenced to prison at fifteen years of age and sent to Patuxent Prison, they had to find a way to get him into a detention facility that would not annihilate his spirit. On the way to have lunch with Jim Rouse, the builder of Columbia, Maryland, and founder of the Rouse Company, Gordon mentioned to Mary that he intended to ask Jim Rouse over lunch for money to pay for their son's legal expenses.

Mary was horrified and asked, "Gordon, what on earth makes you think that it would be appropriate to ask Jim Rouse for money while we are his guests for lunch?"

Gordon responded, "Well, Mary, first of all, I think it is fine to ask him because **he is a free-thinking adult and can say 'no' if that's what is right for him**. He has no trouble saying no. Secondly, **I feel totally unattached to his answer**. If he says yes, that is fine. If he says no, that is equally fine because I trust the money will come from somewhere else, if not from Jim. The third reason I feel it is appropriate is that **helping out in this way might bring Jim joy and create a connection between Jim and our son that could have meaning for both of them**."

We seek to invite others to stand in the gap with Recovery Café, acknowledging everyone's freedom to say no without attachment to their response. This requires staying centered in the reality of abundance—trusting that what is needed will be given—and rooted in the belief that if it is right for them it will bring them joy and deepen community for all involved.

These three principles of fundraising have served us well and given us freedom to invite anyone and everyone we meet to participate in the healing work of Recovery Café. If they do not feel drawn to our mission, we encourage them to find another place to put their weight down—if they have not already done so—and in so doing help close the pain-filled gap in our world.

Another reason we feel relatively free asking people for money is this: we know all of us have a need to give (it is in our DNA) and we know that Recovery Café is an innovative, compassionate, cost-effective, life-transforming response to the needs of many of

Seattle's most vulnerable women and men. If people have a need to give and we can connect them with a powerful response, we are giving them a gift by inviting them to support Recovery Café.

Once I was giving a talk at Recovery Café. The room was full of donors, volunteers and Members of our community. A gentleman slipped in a little late and sat down in the back of the room.

He thought he was in the Alcoholics Anonymous meeting that meets down the hall, where everyone is given *just three minutes* to share. So about five minutes into my fifteen-minute speech, he yelled to me from the back of the room, "Hey windbag, shut up and give someone else a chance to share!" Where else could you receive such immediate, authentic feedback?

Ultimately our fundraising goal is to invite people into authentic relationships with people from radically different socio-economic realities and life experiences.

In the New Testament story of the loaves and fish,

Jesus had been teaching a crowd of people that had grown to about 5,000. At the end of the day, as it was growing dark, Jesus said to his disciples, "Feed the people."

The disciples were taken aback. They said, "With all due respect, we only have five loaves and two fish and there are close to 5,000 people here. Do you expect us to go into town and buy food for 5,000 people?"

Jesus was not fazed by their whining. He was not fazed by their assumption of scarcity. Rooted in a deeper reality, Jesus acted out of an assumption of abundance—an assumption that there is enough to go around.

He instructed his disciples, "Ask the people to sit down in small groups."

Once the people were sitting in small groups—like our Recovery Circles—Jesus said a blessing over the meal. As the story goes, after everyone had been fed there were *baskets full* of food left over.

What if the miracle that happened that day was that once people were seated across from each other and beside each other in small "Recovery Circles," they were able to see each other with new eyes? What if, seeing with new eyes, they were able to drop labels that we all tend to put on each other, labels like liberal or conservative; rich or poor; gay or straight; addict or "normie?"

What if people began to see the individual sitting across from them as not just a mentally ill person or a homeless person or an addicted person or a poor person, or a wealthy person, but as a fellow human being with hopes and dreams just like their own? What if, as stigmas dissolved, people began to dig a little deeper into their backpacks and began to pull out whatever gift they had to share? One brought out a jar of peanut butter, another pulled out a jar of her mother's homemade jam, one dug until he discovered a bruised banana in the bottom of his pack, one pulled out a "Kind bar."

What if the miracle that happened that day was sitting face to face, people began to understand that they were brothers and sisters, members of the same human family? Maybe they began to claim at deeper and deeper levels their oneness with those they once regarded as "strangers" or maybe just "strange."

I am continuously inspired by the way Recovery Café Members share with each other whatever gifts they have to share. Everyone shares the gift of their own story, the ways their lives have been shaped by those who loved them and those who failed to love them the way they needed to be loved. One Member brings in information about a shelter that has openings; another brings in a bag of oranges; another a pair of shoes; another an application for a housing opportunity.

One of our Members received an unexpected inheritance check in the mail from a distant relative, for $10,000. She brought it to David Coffey and me and said, "Since my basic needs are being met—my need for food and housing, health care and community—I want to give this to Recovery Café to help others who are suffering in the ways I used to suffer."

We tried to talk her out of giving the money. We suggested she open up a bank account and save the money for some future emergency, but it became clear to us that her mind was made up. She insisted, "Your needs when you are 'out there' cannot wait."

All of us want more than anything else for our lives to be used for good, for our lives to be a part of creating a more just, compassionate world. All of us want to offer a portion of our gifts and our resources on behalf of the whole community—not just those in our own little biological family. But how do we connect deeply enough with those outside our own little circle of family and friends—with those whose basic needs for food, housing, education and health care are not being met—until their needs become our needs, their suffering becomes our suffering? How do we love deeply enough to become willing to fight for justice and dismantle systems that oppress and exclude those we've come to love?

Rabbi Moshe Leib of Sassov (1745-1807) "learned to love when he went to an inn and heard one drunken peasant ask another, 'Do you love me?' 'Certainly I love you,' replied the second. 'I love you like a brother.' But the first shook his head and insisted, 'You don't love me. You don't know what I lack. You don't know what I need.' The second peasant fell into sullen silence, but Rabbi Moshe Leib understood: 'To know the need of [others] and to bear the burden of [their] sorrow; that is true love.'"

Real relationships are what change us. Real relationships that cross disparate realities free us from the mindset that we are ultimately responsible for our good fortune and that the poor are ultimately responsible for their suffering. Real relationships help us recognize and internalize that there is not a level playing field, and that some are given every opportunity to fulfill their potential while others fight exhausting, personal and systemic, uphill battles, day in and day out from the moment of their conception.

6

ACCOMPANIMENT

We are all just walking each other home.

Ram Dass

FINANCIAL resources are critical to our operations, but the resource of people—staff, volunteers and Members—deeply called and committed to our healing community is by far our most valuable resource.

Eleven years later Ruby Takushi still shapes Recovery Café's evolving, innovative program and holds us to the very best practices in the mental health and substance abuse recovery field. She has a commitment to kindness and excellence that is evident in every dimension of our community's life. Without Ruby's attention to every nuance of our evolving program it simply would not have become a "healing, recovery community" other groups seek to replicate.

Mary Crow still holds us to the essence of Recovery Café's vision to be a community in which we come to know that we are precious and unconditionally loved; come to understand that healing is painful, but possible; and begin to discover that we have gifts to unearth and share with the whole. Everyone's gifts are needed, but the most important gift each person brings to our community is the gift of his or her unique self. When a community is grounded in unconditional love it is possible for that unique, deepest, truest self to be awakened in its members, staff, volunteers and supporters.

"Before his death, Rabbi Zusya said, 'In the coming world, they will not ask me: 'Why were you not Moses?' They will ask me: 'Why were you not Zusya.'"

When our first Director of Operations, Theron Shaw, followed his heart to San Francisco, we wondered where we would ever find someone with his spiritual depth, creativity, intelligence and administrative expertise. We loved Theron, and as a member of New Creation Community he had loved our community from its inception. So we did what we always do: "prayed like it is all up to God and worked like it is all up to us," to find the next person to step into that role.

No one but God, him/herself, could have sent the faithful, servant leader, David Coffey. As Executive Director, David is brilliant at strategizing and relationship building. No one works harder or is as unflappably good-natured. David is the glue that holds together all the dimensions of Recovery Café's work.

Recovery Café is part of a larger movement and we honor the many roles this long-haul work requires. Jo Ann Gibson Robinson played that "glue" role during the Montgomery Bus Boycott. She worked tirelessly, usually behind the scenes. Martin Luther King, Jr. became the public face of the bus boycott, but it was Jo Ann Gibson Robinson, about whom most have never heard, who organized the bus boycott which ignited the civil rights movement. Perhaps the next Jo Ann Gibson Robinson or Martin Luther King, Jr. will emerge from among the women and men who sought out Recovery Café in their darkest hour.

It is not possible in a short narrative to describe every loving individual who has been part of Recovery Café's remarkable community since its inception thirteen years ago. However, Jason Fitzgerald was the gift given during a pivotal time in the life of our community when we more than doubled our capacity and deepened our intentions to meet each Member where they are. Jason came to us with seven years of recovery from a life in which he battled chaos and addiction. He brings the gifts of his own life experience, sharp wit, unusual intelligence, irresistible charisma and commitment to always doing "the most loving thing," which is an essential ingredient in Recovery Café's special sauce.

The most loving thing is a phrase we inherited from Samaritan Inns in Washington, DC and use a lot around Recovery Café. It is a concept at the heart of what we do and who we are in this community. The most loving thing is not a sentimental notion. The most loving thing initially may not feel loving. The most loving thing is a response that is necessary for any of us to "wake up" and take our next step toward healing and transformation. The most loving thing often comes in the form of spoken truths that hold up a mirror so we can see what previously we were not able to see. The most loving thing may come in the form of "loving accountability" that helps us take tangible steps we previously have been unable to take. The most loving thing always holds in tension our concern for the individual and commitment to the well-being of the whole community.

James has an explosive temper that has burned bridges to almost every person and place of support in his life. Recently, when he started to raise his voice within the Café, Jason invited James to take a walk with him to calm down. Outside, Jason spoke the truth to him in love. "You have gotten yourself cut off from almost every place of support in this city. Don't cut yourself off from your community here at the Café. You need us and we need you. Practice reining in that temper. It hurts you and upsets others and we can't allow it." James stormed away from the conversation. Then a block away from the Café, he turned around and yelled loud enough for all in downtown Seattle to hear, "I love you, J! I could kiss you."

Like the eye of a hurricane, right smack in the middle of his emotional storm, James connected with the reality of Jason's love for him and proclaimed his love in return. Jason often tells Members, "If you give up and we lose you, we won't lose just you; we will lose all the lives you will touch and help heal that we haven't even met yet."

Unconventional, compassionate responses emerge daily from our devoted, creative staff, interns, volunteers and the Members themselves. It is not enough simply to remove the destructive behaviors associated with addiction and other mental health challenges without putting something positive in their place. It would be like removing crumbling bricks from a wall without replacing them with solid bricks. Eventually the vacant places where there once were bricks would cause the entire wall to collapse. It is the same with recovery from addiction and other mental health challenges. So we offer a wide array of solid "bricks" in our community to help rebuild stable lives.

Great care is given by the entire team in a weekly consult, led by Ruby, to come up with the most loving, tailor-made response for Members' unique set of challenges and gifts. We rely on our guiding principles and some basic rules, but there is no one-size-fits-all response. As the team grapples with how best to meet people where they are—an ingredient in Recovery Café's special sauce—wise experienced Ruby regularly reminds us, "It depends."

• • •

Ella was not born blind. Moments after her birth a tragic human error took place in a small hospital in Arizona, sentencing her to life in darkness. There were no lawyers representing her poor, bewildered parents and no settlement to serve as a safety net for Ella.

We first learned of Ella through Jamila, a Member of Recovery Café. Jamila worked for the Department of Human Services as a caregiver for the disabled. She discovered Ella living in the pitch black, low-income, apartment unit she was assigned to clean. Ella never left her apartment and was usually drunk when Jamila arrived. Jamila, who brings light to every life she touches, engaged Ella in conversation as she picked up beer cans and threw away half-eaten TV dinners.

As the two women began to develop a friendship, Jamila invited Ella to come with her to Recovery Café. Ella joined a Recovery Circle, attended AA meetings held at Recovery Café and enrolled in classes in the School for Recovery. It may sound cliché, but a light came on inside Ella that shines through the windows of her glass-like eyes when she talks.

Ella was in my Recovery Circle so I had the privilege of hearing the story of her early life and recovery as it unfolded. Ella reported each week, "Since I found this place I don't have anything to complain about." She is economically poor and blind, but rich in friendships and able to see her life as blessed.

Jamila exemplifies the concept of accompaniment. She

literally accompanies Ella to doctor's appointments, to the grocery store and to her Recovery Café community. She is her lifeline. Accompanying Ella comes naturally to Jamila. And as in any authentic relationship, their relationship is mutually liberating. Jamila shared, "I've always blamed myself for my father's abuse of me. Ella has helped me quit making excuses for my abusive father. Until I was able to hold him responsible for the abuse, I was not able to forgive him."

"Ella compares my struggle with my dad to her struggle, saying, 'Being blind is not my fault, but it is my path.'"

• • •

Jackson was so trapped in the darkness of his addiction to crack cocaine that the only escape he could see was jumping off the overpass in front of a semi-truck. He climbed over the stone barriers, waited until he saw the truck approaching, and just as he was about to throw himself into the path of the truck he heard someone yell, "Get Help." Startled by the voice, he looked all around but there was no one in sight.

"The voice made me pause long enough to realize that I didn't really want to die, I just didn't know how to fuckin' live," Jackson recalled.

"I crawled off the barrier and found my way to Harborview Emergency room. Since I no longer wanted to kill myself and had no desire to kill anyone else, they asked me to pee in a cup and sent me, a homeless man, home."

Jackson has been stable in his recovery from addiction, severe depression and post-traumatic stress disorder for nine years. He accompanies seven men and two women as they walk toward stability in housing, relationships, employment and mental, physical and spiritual health. He facilitated a weekly Recovery Circle, one form of accompaniment, but his commitment to his "flock" wasn't limited to the circle. All of the members of his circle were given his phone number and encouraged to call him anytime they needed his support, day or night.

I've observed one of the many ways Jackson supports other community Members. When he knows someone is struggling, he strategically invites members of the larger Recovery Café community to "give Henry or Maria a call today with a few words of encouragement." He keeps love and support circulating throughout our body.

He began accompanying others early in his recovery. Walking with others who were in even more agony or danger than he was became the oxygen that fanned a sputtering spark of life into a full-blown blaze.

It was two days before Christmas, a year after Jackson had crawled down from the overpass. He was having coffee in his bare apartment with a man who was fraught with anxiety over the financial wreckage of his disease. Jackson recalls, "There was no food in my refrigerator and my cabinets were empty. Even though I was a little worried myself, I told this 'sponsee' not to worry. I told him if he would focus on his recovery and follow suggestions, the wreckage of his past would eventually be repaired. While we were still talking, the phone rang. It was a man asking me if he could buy a painting I had done in an art class at Recovery Café, the first painting I'd ever done. He'd seen the painting at the fundraiser. He asked, 'How much do you want for it?' I asked, 'How much do you want to pay?' The caller responded, 'How does $200 sound?' I responded, 'Sounds sold.' It turned out to be a good Christmas after all!"

One afternoon after thanking Jackson for all the gifts he brings to our community, I asked, "Do you know how much I love you?" Grinning from ear to ear, he replied, "I had a sneaking suspicion."

• • •

Once again, reflecting back on our very beginning days in our first space on 2nd and Bell, we hired a social worker to address specific needs like health care, housing and legal aid by setting up appointments and making referrals. We were excited that after all the hoop jumping required by the social service system, Tammy was next on the waiting list for housing. All she had to do was show up at the right time and place. When we learned Tammy didn't show up we were disappointed and frustrated. Mary learned that on her way to the appointment, Tammy had a panic attack. The obstacles on the road to stability in mental health are insurmountable for some during a significant bout with their illness. The illness itself blocks access to treatment. Mary said, "We can't hire a personal social worker to accompany every Member to every appointment, and we don't need that. We need to train Members who have achieved a certain degree of stability in their own recovery from addiction and other mental conditions to accompany Members who are just beginning their journey toward stability."

Delores tends to keep to herself. She is often in a world of her own, creating artistic designs and then carefully coloring the designs. After a series of relapses, Don was about to give up. He was at the end of his rope. Delores noticed Don sitting alone at a corner table and read his despair. Acting against her introverted nature, she approached Don, gently touched his arm and simply said, "Don, I see you."

Sometimes, just being seen as a fellow traveler on life's journey is all we need to show up for another hour or another day.

John Wilson, a Seattle yoga instructor whose loving energy is palpable, recognized how effective yoga is in calming tormented minds and healing post-traumatic stress disorder, from which many of our Members suffer. He began offering a yoga class to Members who otherwise would not be able to afford this healing practice. The interest was so great and the impact so positive on Recovery Café Members that John began training Members to become certified yoga instructors. Currently thirteen Members have been trained and certified. Now yoga classes are offered most mornings at Recovery Café, and most taught by Members of Recovery Café whom John accompanied through the process of training and certification.

A strong commitment to raising up leaders is another ingredient in our special sauce. We have already hosted three, weeklong Recovery Coach trainings, certifying and empowering Members to "walk with" those just beginning the recovery journey, which they have traveled for a longer time. Our hope is to continue to train Members as Recovery Coaches, and eventually be able to pay them for this important work.

Dylan explained, "It was like a nuclear blast went off in my life and there was nothing left. When I could not stand the 'nothingness' any longer, I tried to kill myself."

He continued, "I spent two weeks on the psych ward at University of Washington Hospital. When they released me my friend, Jody, picked me up from the hospital and took me straight to Recovery Café to sign me up for a Recovery Circle. That was two and a half years ago."

Now, Dylan facilitates a weekly Recovery Circle at Recovery Café and serves as a recovery coach for eight individuals with whom he meets one-on-one, weekly, offering them the same support that was his lifeline when he first arrived at Recovery Café. He also works thirty hours a week at a mental health crisis line listening to those devastated by their own "nuclear blasts."

The ripple effect throughout our city and beyond from one person accompanying another is compelling to county and state funders and policy makers. On the state level, Vince Collins, Director of Access to Recovery for Washington State, has been pivotal. Vince has come alongside us with extraordinary encouragement and deep capacity to see the impact this model can make beyond our walls. Policy changes come slowly and government funding can shift from one critical need to another. Of this we are certain, it is in offering our lives for the sake of another's healing that we, ourselves, become whole.

• • •

One of Jamila's earliest childhood memories was being beaten by her father.

"He beat me when he felt I said something stupid. He beat me for wetting the bed. He even beat me for getting beat up by a bully on the playground at school. I wanted to run away from home, but I was afraid the police would just bring me back and I would be beaten for running away."

By the third grade she began to hear voices and became aware of distinct personalities living and arguing in her head. She didn't dare tell anyone about the voices, afraid she'd be accused of being a witch and be beaten for that. "I felt different and isolated. I remember wanting to die. That longing to die—to be relieved of the pain I felt of being so alone—stayed with me for the next fifty years. I began using alcohol to numb the pain."

Jamila got arrested for a traffic violation and ended up

in jail for nine months. Eventually, the court ordered a psychiatric evaluation, and she was diagnosed with post-traumatic stress disorder and schizoaffective disorder. Not long after being released from prison she discovered Recovery Café.

"Recovery Café has helped me stabilize in my recovery from mental illness and addiction. It helped me discover passion for living for the first time in my life. It is a community where I am safe and where I know I belong. It has even helped me forgive my father. I understand now that even though he is dead I must forgive him if I want to be free."

Over the past ten years Jamila has taken almost every course offered in Recovery Café's School for Recovery, including yoga. "I discovered that yoga helped me to go within to a deep, still place and to calm the voices that used to torment me." She entered Recovery Café's teacher training program and became a certified yoga instructor.

"That gave me the opportunity to teach yoga at a

mental health clinic to people who are tormented by voices as I was for most of my life. Thanks to Recovery Café I have a community where I am loved, where I belong and where I contribute to the healing of others. That has given my life purpose and meaning. I would not trade my life today for anyone's."

7

TRANSFORMING TRAUMA

There is no refuge from suffering. But it is also true that suffering has no refuge from love. When love permeates suffering consistently over time, suffering dissolves in love until only love remains.

James Finley

THE multi-dimensional work of Recovery Café could be described as "transforming trauma." By the time most of us have lived very long we get wounded. Some get wounded more often and more profoundly than others. When we get wounded it's as if a layer of scar tissue forms around our core, that place of Divine Love in us that is limitless and transcendent.

Many in our community have experienced trauma. Many suffer from post-traumatic stress disorder. As psychologist and teacher, James Finley, points out, the damage done is not just the trauma which occurred when they were children, but what the trauma continues to do to them each day. It compromises their capacity to be fully present to their lives, their capacity to have compassion for themselves or, in rare cases, for others. It compromises their capacity to use presence and compassion to guide their next steps.

Living with profound wounds can result in emotional pain too intense to hold. Unable to hold the pain we project it onto others, or numb the pain through self-destructive behaviors. Self-destructive behaviors, such as substance abuse, acting out sexually or "dissociative" eating, to name just a few, inevitably create more trauma. Living on the streets of any city inevitably creates more trauma. Loss of health, loss of any sense of self-worth or purpose and meaning creates more trauma. Those who have suffered trauma have lost a sense of the world being a safe place. Our community helps Members begin to trust that even though the world may not be a safe place, there are safe places within the world. Recovery Café seeks to be that safe place where the multiple layers of trauma each person brings are met by unconditional love and over time "dissolve in love until only love remains."

Anne, Wendy, Joan and Kimberly have suffered the trauma of knowing their child's life was at risk due to their addiction and/or mental health challenge and there was absolutely nothing that they, as parents, could do to stop what felt like a freight train speeding toward its demise. As hosts of the Parent Group, they show up each week and lovingly hold a healing space for bewildered parents and other family members.

Although there are no easy answers or quick fixes, these women offer presence and the assurance that whether your hearts are breaking or filled with relief because your child is in recovery now, you are not alone. There is no "us" and "them" in the realities of addiction and mental health challenges.

•   •   •

Maria, barely five feet tall and one hundred pounds, participated in a "transforming trauma" group. She shared with the group that she is there because she has trouble forcing herself to eat. "I've always believed that I'm not worthy of getting to eat, so it is hard for me to eat. I'm trying to force myself to eat something three times a day, but it is really hard to get the food down." Maria regularly shares epiphanies, such as, "I've concluded that Jesus is my brother, the only brother I've ever had who did not sexually abuse me."

One day Maria announced with a proud grin, "I have eaten oatmeal for breakfast every, single day this week."

For many the abuse came in the form of neglect and abandonment. One woman shared, "It would be hard not to conclude that your life doesn't matter when your only parent was gone for days at a time getting high."

The various expressions of community at Recovery Café are the soil in which multiple layers of trauma can be met by love.

Another expression of healing community through which Members steadily reclaim their emotional, psychological, spiritual and physical health is in the Sole Train Walking/Running Club. The idea for a "mobile Recovery Circle" that would help motivate Members to become physically active took off due to the focused energy of our vibrant Jesuit Volunteer, Liz Coz, and passionate community volunteer, Dr. Vicki Allen. It continues to gather momentum thanks to Vicki's unwavering, loving leadership, thanks to our exuberant, always positive Program Manager, Carolyn Dougherty, and thanks to faithful, caring volunteer, Wayne Widdis. These four, who are all love-in-motion, have shaped this expression of "community within community."

After Members show up to walk four times, they are given a brand new pair of running shoes, provided by Brooks. Carolyn took Shaw to the storage area where the running shoes are kept to help him select his size. After deciding on a pair and lacing them up, Shaw started to weep. When he regained composure he explained to Carolyn, "This is the first pair of new shoes I have ever had in my life."

Twice a week Members gather at the front door and hit the pavement together for walks or runs of varying lengths and speeds. They enter road races and fun runs together, carrying a Recovery Café banner, and are met with loud cheers of support along the way. During these outings, muscles are awakened, calories are burned, heart rates are raised, friendships are formed and barriers related to age, race, religion or socio-economic distinctions are dissolved.

8

PITS

Where there is ruin, there is hope for treasure.

Rumi

The greatest glory in living lies not in never falling, but in rising every time we fall.

Nelson Mandela

I do not at all understand the mystery of grace—only that it meets us where we are but does not leave us where it found us.

Anne Lamott

ABOUT seventeen years ago I suffered a trauma that plunged me into a pit of depression. At that time I had already worked in the mental health field for fifteen years, so I had an intellectual understanding of what I was experiencing. But no matter how hard I tried, I could not pull myself out of that pit. It took a loving community made up of friends, family, a counselor, and those who were working through similar challenges to pull me out of that pit.

I'll never forget what one friend said to me during that dark period. She said:

> *Right now you have lost your capacity to imagine, to hope and to trust. I will be your imagination during this time. I will hold the hope for your complete recovery. I will trust for you that this experience will be used for good.*

That experience, which I never would have chosen,

profoundly deepened my commitment to this work and helped shape the healing community Recovery Café has become. And I have had the immense privilege of imagining, hoping and trusting on behalf of many who were trapped in their own deep pits and could not get out on their own.

In the Spring of 2014, while hiking with friends in a remote rain forest, I fell an estimated thirty feet into a sink hole, shattering my right leg and my left foot, and suffering other trauma related injuries. Immediately, without saying a word to anyone, a member of the group who had grown up in that part of the world scaled the rock-face down into the pit, scooped me up into his arms and then began the arduous process of getting me out of that pit. He would bench press me a couple of feet, perch my body on a jutting rock and then bench press me a couple of more feet.

By the time we were about halfway from the bottom of the pit, the guide of our hike crawled down into the pit and met us. When he saw that I was alive and conscious, he yelled exuberantly to members of our group who had gathered at the top of the pit, "I can't believe she's alive!" His announcement, which alerted me to the fact that there was some question about my being alive, prompted me to lose consciousness.

When I regained consciousness, the guide, touching my toes, asked if I could feel him touching my toes. I had to concentrate, then mumbled, "Yes." Once again, he yelled exuberantly to those gathered around the top, this time announcing, "I can't believe she's not paralyzed!" Once again his announcement prompted my immediate loss of consciousness. Turns out, you are not supposed to let on just how hurt someone is during the rescue.

When I was about four feet from the top of the pit, they allowed Bernie to crawl down and cradle my head in his arms. I was still in and out of consciousness, but I remember Bernie lovingly, repeatedly urging me, "Stay with us, Killian."

An extraordinary surgeon, hospital and health care

professionals, praying community, faithful friends bringing presence and presents, nutritious meals, and grace heaped upon grace put me back together again.

Having experienced two different kinds of pits, one thing I know for sure is that **no one gets out of a deep pit on their own.**

All of the Members of Recovery Café have at some point found themselves in the deep, dark pit of addiction and/or some other mental illness. But for eleven years the supporters, board, staff, partners, volunteers and Members of Recovery Café, have refused to walk past women and men suffering at the bottom of that pit. They heard their cries, allowed their hearts to be broken by the anguish, carefully climbed into the pit alongside them, cradled them in their arms and then—love lifted thousands of women and men who thought they had been left for dead.

They understood that for many the fall to the dark bottom of the pit began with early childhood abuse and that the climb out of the pit requires more than a few expensive hours in an emergency room during a mental health crisis or an appointment with a mental health professional once every four to seven weeks.

They understood what is essential for healing of multiple trauma wounds is a place where we experience being deeply known and loved; a place where we can serve, grow, contribute to the healing of others, develop our own gifts and fulfill our God-given potential.

The second thing I know from falling in a pit is that life can change in an instant. You can be strolling along—not paying attention—and in an instant your life can be totally different than it was before. Time is not promised to any of us. The wise learn from their time in the pit to live each day with the same compassion, generosity and presence they would choose to live if they knew it was their last day.

Only what we do for love will last beyond our brief lives. Our relentless pursuit of things and sensation may numb our existential despair, but it does not bring us lasting joy.

The third thing I know from time in a pit is that everyone either has already—or will at some point—experience time in a pit. Maybe that pit was or will be a painful divorce, a traumatic betrayal, a life-altering illness. Maybe that pit was or will be the loss of a job or the loss of a dream. We don't usually get to choose the pit we find ourselves in, but we *can* choose our response. We can choose to become *bitter or better.* We can allow our pain to shut down our hearts or break our hearts wide open.

If we allow it all the things in our life we would never have chosen can make us more aware of our deep connection to every member of the human family. If we allow it, our time in whatever pit we find ourselves can result in our becoming contributors to the healing of others.

Jenni was sexually abused by her older brother, which resulted in her becoming pregnant at age fourteen. Her parents sent her to a home for, as then referred to, unwed mothers. Some of the other "girls" in the home introduced her to an array of illegal drugs. She spent the next seventeen soul-scorching years addicted to heroin and methamphetamines.

As she discovered healing and stability in Recovery Café's community she began to ask, "What gifts do I have that could be used to help others?" One day she excitedly concluded, "As an intravenous drug user I was awesome at finding veins." So she enrolled in a medical technicians' program, trained to be a phlebotomist and graduated as the best in her class at finding veins and drawing blood.

Last month, she drove to Yakima, Washington, to confront her brother for the years of abuse and to say, "I want you to get on with your life and I want to get on with mine, so I forgive you."

If we allow it, even our brokenness, our failures and our disasters can be used for good.

• • •

As a society, a common fear-based response to women and men suffering in the deep pit of homelessness, addiction and other mental health challenges is "out of sight, out of mind." A Department of Justice study found that seventy-five percent of women and fifty percent of men in state penitentiaries, and seventy-five percent of women and sixty-three percent of men in local jails, suffer from a mental health condition.

Not only is it cruel to imprison rather than treat those with mental illness, it is costly. According to the Executive Director of the Global Mental Health Program of Columbia University, "Mental illness is the leading cause of disability worldwide. It costs more to ignore mental illness than to treat it. When we fail to treat people who suffer from mental disorders like schizophrenia, bipolar disorder, addiction and major depression, we all lose. The economic burden of associated health problems, lost productivity and lost lives is more than ten times the budgets now being spent to treat people with mental illness." This is totally unacceptable. We must do better. And we can do better, because models of cost-effective, compassionate, healing, recovery communities like Recovery Café, already exist. We must build on that foundation.

• • •

Gordon Cosby devoted the last seventy years of his life to changing systems that exclude the poor and creating structures that bring healing and hope in Washington, DC. A couple of months before his death I went to DC to spend time with him. He told me about his latest initiative, the creation of a micro-lending organization in DC for those trapped in poverty.

Gordon shared, "I kept sensing I was being called to this new vision, so I prayed, 'God, I am a ninety-five-year-old man who can barely stand up. I can't lead this initiative.'

"But I felt God's response to me was, 'Gordon, you still

have influence. Use whatever influence you have for the suffering poor.'"

Gordon understood, all that is not given is lost: only what we invest in love lasts beyond our brief lives on this earth.

9

OUTSIDERS
NO MORE

There are few things more devastating than to have it burned into you that you do not count… This sense of powerlessness is key to the maintenance of any system of economic, racial, [gender] and social control; a system in which some have been disinherited.

Howard Thurman

JESUS tells the story of a man who has been robbed, beaten up and left to die on the side of the road and of two different responses to that man's needs. The first response is that of the religious authorities. They both cross the street and walk away from the suffering.

The second response comes from a Samaritan, one who knows what it is like to live as an outsider on the margins of a culture. The Samaritan stops, administers first aid, transports the victim to an inn and arranges to pay for his ongoing health care.

Perhaps the religious authorities were just too busy doing many good things to even notice the suffering man. Or perhaps their crossing to the other side of the street had more to do with feeling overwhelmed by the severity of this man's need and feeling inadequate to make an effective response. Most of us can relate to either or both of those responses.

But something else is going on in this story. The religious authorities were responsible for maintaining a kind of religious caste system, known as the purity system. Biblical scholar Marcus Borg explains that in the purity system of first century Judaism people were categorized according to varying degrees of purity, moving from the very pure at the center—the bull's eye—to those on the margins of purity, to those considered radically impure—the untouchables. One's status in the purity system depended to a large degree on birth, economic stability, gender, religion, race, physical and mental well-being and how well one observed the requirements of the system.

The religious authorities were considered very pure and at the center. In the next circle would fall generally religious men. Women—who were considered much less pure than men—would have been in one of the outer circles, followed by tax collectors, shepherds, the poor and the maimed. Then there were those considered so impure they were not even on the purity system's map at all, those like Samaritans, lepers, people who were bleeding and people who were considered impure from having touched a dead body.

In order for these first century religious authorities to stop and embrace a man rendered impure because he was bleeding and half-dead, they would have had to be willing to confront not only the suffering of one outside their circle, but the system they were at the heart of, a system of which they were the primary beneficiaries.

• • •

John was a member of Recovery Café for two years. After establishing a foundation in recovery from homelessness, bipolar disorder and alcoholism he pursued a degree at Seattle University. As a student he had access to health care, which paid for his prescription meds.

At Recovery Café he had a community where he was deeply known and loved; a structure of loving accountability that reinforced care for body, mind and spirit; and support from others who understood the complexity and challenges of co-occurring disorders. He started walking everyday and lost fifty-two pounds. He was engaged intellectually in his courses. He meditated every day. He was funny and fully alive.

When he graduated he no longer had access to health care and could not afford his medication. After about two months off his medication his mental health took a nosedive and he began to self-medicate with alcohol. He quit showing up for his Recovery Circle and quit responding to friends via e-mail and text. Bart, another friend of John's, and I, decided to show up at his apartment. We knocked and knocked and knocked but there was no response. Reluctantly we called 911.

While working in DC I had witnessed a 911 call that resulted in the traumatized person being slammed, facedown on the pavement, handcuffed and treated like a criminal, when his only crime was that he was desperately ill. But when these Seattle first responders got into John's apartment and discovered he was in mental health crisis, or "collapse," they treated him with gentleness and respect.

As they loaded him into the ambulance John sobbed, "Killian, I never wanted you to see me like this." The profound shame he felt over being desperately ill broke my heart.

We trusted John was in good hands and planned to check in with him the next morning at the hospital. But John was not admitted to the hospital. We do not know all the reasons he was not admitted. What we do know is that he was released to the streets and before morning came he was dead.

I have gone over the events leading up to John's death over and over in my mind. At every step of the way, Recovery Café did the most loving thing for John; at every point we made a compassionate response. It is easy for non-profits like Recovery Café to become consumed by the needs of the women and men we serve and to accept that our compassionate responses to those needs are enough. However, when we focus our energy entirely on compassionate responses, we run the risk of ignoring the underlying assumptions and systems at the root of so much poverty and injustice in America.

Our focus on compassionate responses must not result in our allowing city, state and federal governments to shirk responsibility for guaranteeing affordable housing, healthcare for physical and mental health conditions, decent education, living wages and a criminal justice system that is, in fact, just.

In her book *Sweet Charity,* sociologist Janet Poppendieck writes that charity can act as "a sort of moral safety valve; it can reduce the discomfort evoked by visible destitution in our midst by creating the illusion of effective action and offering us myriad ways of participating in it. It can create a culture of charity that normalizes destitution and legitimates personal generosity as the only response [to injustice]."

Compassionate responses are critical, but they are not enough. Compassionate responses and confrontation of unjust systems responsible for growing inequality must go together; they are two sides of the same coin.

David Hilfiker, a member of Eighth Day Church, one of the Church of the Saviour communities, author, and founder of Joseph's House, a hospice for people dying of AIDS and other terminal illnesses, wrote: "We hear so much talk these days about 'faith-based' [or non-profit] organizations as appropriate tools for dealing with social ills—perhaps even replacing government as the primary provider of services to the needy. But while they certainly play a useful role they cannot be a substitute for government. Only the government—that is 'we the people,' acting in concert locally, statewide and nationally—can guarantee rights, can create or oversee programs that assure everyone adequate access to the most basic needs."

For sure, a healthy debate is necessary about how government can most effectively address these basic needs. But without a commitment from both government and caring people—without public and private partnerships–the gap between those who have what they need to fulfill their potential and live healthy lives and those who do not will continue to widen.

Take for example the civil rights movement in the 1950's and 60's. Mostly African American activists risked their lives making non-violent, compassionate responses to the immense suffering of black people, but it was critical for those compassionate responses to be encoded into law–for those rights to be guaranteed by government, in order for a significant shift to occur in the deplorable inequality.

Obviously more shifts toward equality are needed in our country. These shifts need to be encoded into law and guaranteed by government, as well. In short, it is not enough for us to simply be concerned about specific needs of the poor in our country such as homelessness or hunger.

These are symptoms. We must be willing to look underneath the hood at injustice. Injustice is the result of any system or structure in our society–economic, governmental, social and, yes, religious–that undergirds inequality.

Out of 2.3 million inmates in the United States:

Eighty percent are poor.

Sixty percent are members of a racial and ethnic minority even though racial and ethnic minorities make up only twenty-three percent of the general population.

Bryan Stevenson of the Equal Justice Initiative, writes, "We have a system in which you are treated better if you are rich and guilty than if you are poor and innocent."

In *Long Walk to Freedom*, Nelson Mandela wrote: "It is said that no one truly knows a nation until one has been inside its jails. A nation should not be judged by how it treats its highest citizens, but its lowest ones." There are ten times more women and men with mental illness in our prisons than in our psychiatric hospitals.

Our deep desire is that Recovery Café will give teeth to the compelling argument–which is gaining steam–against criminalizing women and men suffering from the disease of addiction and other mental health challenges and against throwing people away through long draconian mandatory sentencing.

Our deep desire is that the Recovery Café model will somehow be used to help create caring, compassionate, healing communities in every town and city across the U.S. and beyond and that we will help erase the stigma and shame surrounding mental illness. Our deep desire is that city, state and federal governments will commit to longer-term, compassionate communities as the "new normal" in how we treat the addicted and mentally ill in this country and that they will be willing to invest greater resources to that end.

The Director of the White House National Drug Control Policy, President Obama's "drug czar," Michael Botticelli, visited Recovery Café. We were struck by his caring, gentle spirit, which seemed incongruent with the need for the armed federal Marshals who accompanied him. Normally you are not allowed to enter Recovery Café if you are "packing."

The Director asked: "How did you know to create a long-term, healing community over ten years before the research would indicate how crucial long-term communities are in addressing addiction and co-occurring disorders?" Everyone needs a place to heal when they are desperately ill. Everyone needs authentic community where they are known and loved. Everyone needs some structure of loving accountability if they are to become all they were created to become.

Thich Nhat Hanh, the Buddhist Monk nominated by Martin Luther King, Jr. for the Nobel Peace Prize during the Vietnam war, wrote: "Building communities that practice understanding, loving-kindness and compassion may be the most important thing we can do for the survival of our world."

In November 2014, Recovery Café convened a group of outstanding organizations from around Washington State committed to increasing "recovery capital." Many of these organizations had already formed alliances in their own regions, but this state-wide coalition, Washington Recovery Alliance, is a vehicle for sharing best practices, advocating for needed legislation and systemic change and supporting the creation of more compassionate communities for suffering women and men throughout our state.

Recently I have been feeling overwhelmed and at a total loss for what our next steps should be in confronting a criminal justice system that is biased in measurable and specific ways against the poor and people of color, and imprisons more mentally ill people than are currently being treated in psychiatric hospitals across the U.S. Emmy reassured me, "Killian, we have never known what our next steps should be and yet they have always been given."

• • •

Grinding poverty, homelessness, addiction and other mental health challenges, along with sporadic health care, takes years off a person's life.

The Washington Community Mental Health Council reports, "Those with serious mental illness experience more chronic medical problems and have a life expectancy twenty-five years shorter than the general population." And homeless people have a life expectancy of thirty years less than the general population.

Inevitably, Recovery Café provides loving, healing community for many Members during the last years, months and days of their lives. This past winter a Member of our community died each week for four weeks in a row. We did what we are committed to doing—we honored each one in death just as we had honored each one in life.

When a Member dies we place a framed photo and a

battery "candle" in a special place to the right of the front door along with an announcement of the day and time of that Member's memorial service. All gather in a circle and share memories of the one who is no longer with us in body, but whose spirit is a part of us, always.

Cynthia was a tenderhearted, talkative redhead who had been an integral part of our community for eight years. During that time she suffered an abusive marriage and several relapses, but she always returned with an open heart and much love to give. One day she discovered her brother dead on the floor of the apartment they shared with the needle still in his arm. She never recovered from that loss. Her mental illness and addiction raged out of control. She became paranoid and isolated. I called and left messages on her machine, saying, "Come home to us." Various Members went to her apartment, knocked on her door and pleaded with her from outside the door. She was too ashamed to respond.

Listening to my office voicemail on a Wednesday afternoon, Cynthia's voice ripped my heart in two. She had left several messages asking, "Can you call me? I need to talk. I love you." I learned from another Member that not too long after she left those messages, Cynthia died of an overdose, just like her brother.

The community gathered to grieve and remember all the love and laughter she had brought us, to honor her in death, just as we had honored her in life.

Oscar had worked as a chef in a local restaurant until he suffered a stroke and severe memory loss. Because he could no longer hold down a job, he became more and more isolated and depressed. One of our Members invited him to explore being a part of Recovery Café's community. Oscar became a fixture in our kitchen helping to prepare meals each day and sharing food preparation techniques with other Members. Despite his memory impairment he could still play chess and challenged almost everyone in the community to a match. He spent hours each day chopping vegetables in the kitchen and concentrating on games of chess. Then another stroke took his life. None of us had any way of knowing that his months with us would be the last months of his life.

At his memorial service there was an outpouring of love and gratitude for all he had brought to our community. Person after person confessed that Oscar had beat them in chess and countless others spoke of all he taught them in the kitchen. Everyone spoke of his gentle, kind spirit. He died financially poor, but rich in community and purpose.

Honoring community Members after their death not only helps us remember and grieve, but it also reinforces for the living that our lives matter and we will not be forgotten.

10

HOPE

Life is hard, at times as hard as crucible steel. It has its bleak and difficult moments of drought and its moments of flood... If one will hold on, he will discover that God walks with him... God is able to lift you from the fatigue of despair to the buoyancy of hope, and transform dark and desolate valleys into sunlit paths of inner peace.

Martin Luther King, Jr.

Do those things that incline you toward the big questions, and avoid the things that would reduce you and make you trivial. That luminous part of you that exists beyond personality – your soul, if you will – is as bright and shining as any that has ever been. Bright as Shakespeare's, bright as Gandhi's, bright as Mother Teresa's. Clear away everything that keeps you separate from this secret luminous place. Believe it exists, come to know it better, nurture it, share its fruits tirelessly.

George Saunders

SARINA remembers sitting in an alley off Lake City Way praying as hard as she could, asking God to just take her out. She thoroughly believed she'd seen enough of this life and was ready to throw in the towel.

"I had given up on every dream I'd ever had and lost all hope for the future. I couldn't think past getting my next drink or drug. It felt so horrible to admit that I had become everything I said I'd never become, homeless and drug-addicted."

She grew up on the Reservation and spent her entire youth in tribal Foster Care. Her mother, who was an alcoholic, lost Sarina and her sister to Child Protective Services several times and eventually lost her parental rights. She was told that if she ever wanted to see them again the girls would need to live with family and their case transferred to tribal foster care.

"Almost everyone in my family was addicted to drugs or alcohol. My uncle that I went to live with died of an overdose when I was twelve. I had never seen anyone actually recover from addiction. I didn't believe it was possible. I said what a lot of people say who come from broken homes, poverty and hardship… that I would be different."

That is easier said than done. As life's challenges got heavier Sarina turned to the things that temporarily helped her deal with life and made her feel better. Soon she was drinking and using every day. The drugs got progressively worse as did her circumstances.

Eventually, at twenty-one, Sarina ended up in her fourth treatment center. "A friend I met in treatment told me about the Recovery Café. We were supposed to meet there a day after I got out. She never showed up. The transitional housing I moved into was far from drug and alcohol-free. The Café was the only clean and sober environment available to me, the only place I felt safe."

Through 12-step meetings Sarina developed bonds with a core group of friends who were also in recovery. Through those friendships, she began to believe that recovery might be possible for her too. Even though the last thing she wanted was to live in a house full of women, she interviewed for a space in a house for women because it was drug and alcohol-free housing. The women voted her into the house and "before I knew it the final piece of my foundation for recovery was put into place."

"One night my purse was stolen with my house key in it and one of the women made a key for me. As she handed it to me she said, 'This is your home. You need a key for your home.' Those words touched something deep inside me. This began my journey of healing and recovery."

Today, Sarina lives one day at a time with five years of sobriety. She is a full-time student, majoring in business at the University of Washington, and was hired to facilitate events and advocacy for all Native American students on campus.

"Last summer I traveled to Ghana. I was there on my fourth sobriety birthday. I remember sitting quietly and trying to make sense of it all. The best answer I could come up with for such a transformation is that I have not done any of it alone. I could have never imagined I would ever have an incredible opportunity like that."

Her life today still has its challenges. Her sobriety didn't get everyone else in her family sober. "I have thought for a long time that no one in my family cared to notice all the work I've put into changing my life... until recently."

Sarina was going into a 12-step meeting after a long day. It was a particularly hard day, and she was questioning her recovery and feeling unsure of the person she was becoming. "Out of nowhere my mom walked up. She had been drinking and was on her way to go sleep on the church stairs (the same church the meeting was in). I was so happy to see her and began telling her how I was feeling. We talked for a few minutes and split ways. Before leaving she gave me a big hug and told me to go in that meeting and 'represent for all of us.'"

Sarina is still the only one in her family who is drug and alcohol-free. Her purpose today is not to get someone else sober but simply to be an example of what is possible. She has accomplished a lot in the last few years, "but the most important of those accomplishments is that today I know peace; today I look in the mirror and am happy with the person I see; today I am useful in the lives of others and have hope for the future."

You can see why being a part of a community where I get to love and learn from courageous people like Sarina gives me hope and why "the re-birth of a human being makes all the weight of daily life in community worthwhile."

AUTHOR'S NOTE

Recovery Café grew out of a community rooted in the teachings of Jesus. However, this model could be replicated by any community deeply committed to the truth that all people are precious, worthy of unconditional love and deserving of opportunities to heal and fulfill their potential.

If you are interested in starting a healing community in your town or city as an alternative to the imprisonment and abandonment of women and men suffering from homelessness, addiction and other mental health challenges, our community would love to support you in that quest. Please contact us at Recovery Café.

SharingOurModel@recoverycafe.org

www.recoverycafe.org

NEW CREATION
COMMUNITY
CALL AND COMMITMENTS

The Call

To be an intentional, ecumenical, faith community in which the inward and outward journeys are held together. The inward journey involves us in an ever deepening, authentic engagement with self, with God and with others. The inward journey, taken seriously, leads to the discovery of the outward journey, the place our gifts and brokenness connect with a need in the world.

The Commitments

To spend a specific amount of time each day in prayer/meditation, reflection on scripture or other spiritual literature—beginning with ten minutes and moving to one hour or more each day;

To share resources of time and money with the suffering through proportional giving;

To show up weekly for worship and deepening of relationships with the community;

To show up weekly for loving accountability, holding each other to our spiritual commitments, practicing honesty and forgiveness, allowing ourselves to be known deeply, sharing not only our gifts, but also our brokenness, the places where we struggle;

To support each other through prayer and actions as we seek to be faithful to the deepest calls on our lives;

To practice care for our bodies, minds and spirits and to support each other through prayer and loving accountability as we seek to be healthy in body, mind and spirit;

To nurture authentic relationship(s) with someone (or some group) who is oppressed or excluded by the dominant culture and to stand with those who are oppressed or excluded in some specific way, following the example of Jesus, until their struggles become our struggles;

To practice nonviolence in all relationships—both public and private—including relationships with the natural world;

To spend at least one extended period of silence per year as a community;

To leave the community, not out of anger, frustration or disappointment, but when it is discerned, along with the community, that I am no longer called to this community.

SOURCES

Chapter 1: Story Before the Story

Cosby, N. Gordon. From Forword, *Search for Silence*, by Elizabeth O'Connor (San Diego: LuraMedia, 1986).

Chodron, Pema. *Start Where You Are: A Guide to Compassionate Living* (Boston: Shambhala Publications, 1995).

Merton, Thomas, transl. *The Wisdom of the Desert* (New York: New Directions Books, 1960).

Armstrong, Karen. *The Spiral Staircase: My Climb Out of Darkness* (New York: Anchor Books, 2004).

L'Engle, Madeleine. *The Summer of the Great-Grandmother* (New York: Harper Collins, 1974).

Chapter 2: Hearts Broken Open

Salzberg, Sharon. From www.sharonsalzberg.com blog (Web: 2014).

Campbell, Sr. Simone, quoting Dorothy Day in inaugural *Dorothy Day Lecture*, Emmanuel College (Boston: 2014).

Chapter 3: We Belong to Each Other

Tolstoy, Leo. *My Religion* (New York: Thomas Y. Crowell & Co., 1884).

Quotes by Mother Teresa. From www.fulleryouthinstitute.org (Web: 2015).

Vanier, Jean. *From Brokenness to Community* (New Jersey: Paulist Press, 1992).

Kuntz, Ernest, and Katherine Ketcham. *Experiencing Spirituality: Finding Meaning Through Storytelling* (New York: Penguin Books, 2014).

O'Connor, Elizabeth. *The New Community* (New York: Harper & Row, 1976).

Chapter 4: Radical Hospitality

Nouwen, Henri J.M. *Reaching Out: The Three Movements of the Spiritual Life* (New York: Doubleday, 1975).

Maté, Gabor. *In the Realm of Hungry Ghosts: Close Encounters with Addiction* (Berkeley: North Atlantic Books, 2008).

Kierkegaard, Søren. *Sickness Unto Death* (Princeton: Princeton University Press, 1983. First published 1849).

Vanier, Jean. *Letters to L'Arche* (www.larcheusa.org: Fall 2003).

De Mello, Anthony. *Awareness: The Perils and Opportunities of Reality* (New York: Doubleday, 1992).

Chapter 5: Mutually Liberating Relationships

Shaw, George Bernard. *Man and Superman: A Comedy and a Philosophy* (Cambridge, Mass: The University Press, 1903; New York: Bartleby.com, 1999).

Kuntz, Ernest, and Katherine Ketcham. *Experiencing Spirituality: Finding Meaning Through Storytelling* (New York: Penguin Books, 2014).

Chapter 6: Accompaniment

Dass, Ram and Paul Gorman. *How Can I Help? Stories and Reflections on Service* (New York: Alfred A. Knopf, 1999).

Buber, Martin. *Tales of the Hasidim* (New York: Schocken Book, 1975. First published 1947).

Chapter 7: Transforming Trauma

Finley, James. *Spirituality of Healing: Transforming Trauma* (CD, Published by Contemplative Life Bookstore, 2014) http://www.contemplative-life.org/james-finley/spirituality-of-healing-james-finley-cd-or-dvd/.

Chapter 8: Pits

Rumi, Melvana Jelalu'ddin. www.goodreads.com/quotes. (b. 1207, d. 1273).

Mandela, Nelson. *New York Times*, Mandela, at White House, by James Bennet, Quote Page A26, New York.1998 September 23.

Lamott, Anne. *Traveling Mercies: Some Thoughts on Faith* (New York: Anchor Books, 1999).

Department of Justice study, http://www.citizensforcriminaljustice.net/mentally-ill-inmates-are-routinely-physically-abused-study-says/.

Global Mental Health Program, Executive Director Kathy Pike, Columbia University (2013). http://www.cugmhp.org/exec-director-kathy-pikes-comment-new-york-times.

Chapter 9: Outsiders No More

Thurman, Howard. *Jesus and the Disinherited* (Boston: Beacon Press, 1976).

Borg, Marcus. *Meeting Jesus Again for the First Time* (New York: HarperCollins Publishers, 1994).

Poppendieck, Janet. *Sweet Charity?: Emergency Food and the End of Entitlement* (New York: Penguin Books, 1999).

Hilfiker, David. "When Charity Chokes Justice," *The Other Side*, September/October 2002.

Stevenson, Bryan. *Just Mercy: A Story of Justice and Redemption* (New York: Spiegel & Grau, 2014).

Mandela, Nelson. *Long Walk to Freedom: The Autobiography of Nelson Mandela* (Boston: Little, Brown and Company, 1994).

Washington Community Mental Health Council, Hope, Treatment, Recovery (Seattle) http://www.wcmhcnet.org/documents/HopeTreatmentRecovery.pdf.

Chapter 10: Hope

King, Martin Luther, Jr. *Eulogy for the Young Victims of the Sixteenth Street Baptist Church Bombing* (Birmingham, Alabama, 1963).

Saunders, George. Convocation Speech, Syracuse University, May 11, 2014. http://6thfloor.blogs.nytimes.com/2013/07/31/george-saunderss-advice-to-graduates/?_r=0.

Vanier, Jean. *Community and Growth* (Toronto: Griffin House, 1979).

ABOUT THE PUBLISHER

inward/outward offers writings about the spiritual journey in community–inward, into the depths of the true self, and outward, into the depths of the world. A project of The Church of the Saviour, *inward/outward* provides:

- Excerpts to educate and inspire;
- Reflections on scripture;
- Writings from The Church of the Saviour community.

To subscribe or to learn more, visit us:
www.inwardoutward.org
www.facebook.com/inwardoutward